The Hidden Power of Your Words

The Hidden Power of Your Words

Dr. Christian Harfouche

Power House Publishers
Pensacola, Florida

Unless otherwise indicated, all scriptural quotations are from the *King James Version* of the Bible.

Hidden Power of Your Words
Published by:
Power House Publishers
2411 Executive Plaza Rd
Pensacola, FL 32504
ISBN 0-9634451-3-8
www.globalrevival.com

Second Printing, June 2000

Cover design and book production by:
DB & Associates Design & Distribution
dba Double Blessing Productions
P.O. Box 52756, Tulsa, OK 74152
www.doubleblessing.com

Editorial Consultant: Phyllis Mackall, Broken Arrow, Oklahoma

Printed in the United States of America.

Contents

The Hidden Power of Your Words

Chapter 1
Speech: Man's Unique Gift

God has deposited in you the ability to release dynamite-filled, power-packed capsules of expression that we call "words."

The Bible says, "Let us make man in our image, after our likeness: and let them have dominion..." (Genesis 1:26).

God started off giving man dominion over the fish of the sea and the fowl of the air, and He ended up giving man dominion "over *all* the earth."

Then the Bible says, "And the Lord God formed man of the dust of the ground, and breathed into his nostrils the breath of life; and man became a living soul" (Genesis 2:7).

Ever since that moment, mankind has been able to express their nature, perception, heart, desire, vision, and plans *through words*.

These words are alive, and there is not one person who does not have the ability to use words, unless he or she is physically impaired.

Words will cause you either to go higher or to drown deeper. For example, if you're shipwrecked in the ocean, and you see a ship, you can either call out for a lifesaver or an anchor. Whatever you ask for will be what you get. If you call for an anchor, you will go under. Why? Because you asked for the wrong thing!

So God has given us the ability to express our innermost intentions and desires through a unique, power-packed

1

method called speech. However, we are responsible for every word we speak.

Jesus Warns of "Idle Words"

Jesus said, "...every idle word that men shall speak, they shall give account thereof in the day of judgment" (Matthew 12:36). The phrase "idle word" means a non-productive, non-active, ineffective word that does not operate in conjunction with and for the enhancement of the kingdom of God.

Any word that does not cooperate with God's Word — any word that does not cooperate with the will of God for you or the plan of heaven for your destiny — is idle, non-productive, inactive, and unemployed. It means that God did not send that word.

The Bible says, "He sent his word, and healed them" (Psalm 107:20). The Bible does not say, "God sent His Word and made them sick," or, "He sent His Word and beat them up." No. If you've got a word that beats you up, it was not sent by God.

Whenever words are sent by God, they pack power! Jesus said, "the words that I speak unto you, they are *spirit*, and they are *life*" (John 6:63). We are told in Proverbs 18:21, "*Death* and *life* are in the power of the tongue."

We Can Know God's Will

We live in an hour when great opportunities have been granted to us, because we know more of the will of God than Christians have ever known before. There has never been a generation in human history that has had the access to God's will that we do today.

Great men and women of God in past generations have spoken forth revelations from God, and these revelations have been preserved in books, records, tapes, and videotapes, so none of us has an excuse for not knowing what God's will is, let alone for not speaking the perfect will of God for our lives.

God has given us the ability to express ourselves through what we say. He has also given us the ability to block off, reject, and not receive what we hear. He has even given us the ability to hear His Word and not do anything about it!

But, thank God, He has also given us the ability to hear the Word, believe it, declare it, and act on it. And when we do that, we will become the most powerful breed that has ever existed! We will become a brand-new breed of men and women, because we have been born again.

No Longer Mere Mortals

We will no longer be mere mortals walking around, blinded by the god of this world, for we are brand-new creatures who have been created in Christ Jesus unto good works.

Second Corinthians 4:6,7 says:

For God, who commanded the light to shine out of darkness, hath shined in our hearts, to give the light of the knowledge of the glory of God in the face of Jesus Christ.

But we have this treasure in earthen vessels, that the excellency of the power may be of God, and not of us.

Just a few verses before, the apostle Paul had said:

But if our Gospel be hid [if God's Word is hid, if the words God has spoken through the prophets are hid], **they are hid to them that are lost:**

In whom the god of this world hath blinded the minds of them which believe not, lest the light of the glorious gospel of Christ, who is the image of God, should shine unto them.

2 Corinthians 4:3,4

A Question Straight From the Garden of Eden

There is one particular diabolical method the devil uses — and has always used — to blind the minds of men, and that's through words. He'll ask people exactly what he asked Eve in the Garden of Eden: *"Hath God said?"* He'll ask them, "How do you *know* Jesus is the way to God?" He'll ask,

3

"How do you *know* you're going to get anything from God?" He'll ask, "How do you *know* God means you when He gives a promise?"

Notice this about the devil: *If you take his mouth away, you've taken his power away!* He's a dragon. He's going to breathe fiery words to you that are nothing but lies. He's a wolf. He's going to use his mouth to devour the sheep, if he can. He's as a roaring lion seeking whom he may devour. *He's using his mouth to find himself a candidate for defeat!*

So Satan uses his mouth against you. And he blinds the minds of people who don't believe. Why don't they believe? Because they believed the devil rather than God. They heard an evil report and believed it.

When God Speaks

If you believe, it's because you heard a *good* report and believed it. We just read in Second Corinthians about the God who *commanded* the light to shine out of darkness. We serve a commanding God; a God who speaks commands.

Genesis 1:3 says, "And God *said*, Let there be light: and there was light." The original Hebrew text says, "And God said, 'Let there become light,' and light became."

This shows us something. When God speaks words, they are spirit and they are life! When He sends a capsule of Spirit-filled words, the spirit and life in those words explode to carry out His will and His plan. We see an example of this in the first chapter of John's Gospel:

In the beginning was the Word, and the Word was with God, and the Word was God.

The same was in the beginning with God.

All things were made by him, and without him [the Word] was not any thing made that was made.

In him was life; and the life was the light of men.

And the light shineth in darkness; and the darkness comprehended it not.

John 1:1-5

Why couldn't the darkness overcome the light? When you admit even a tiny bit of light into a dark place, you can still see. All you need is one candle in a dark room and the darkness cannot overcome it. Light cannot be extinguished by darkness, but darkness can be blasted by light!

The Light of the World

As we read, the Bible says that "God, who commanded the light to shine...hath shined in our hearts." Why did God shine in my heart? Not so I could sing a little song about "This little light of mine; I'm gonna let it shine."

That's not why He shined. The light that shined in our hearts is not "that little light," because He said, "Ye are the light of the world. A city that is set on an hill cannot be hid" (Matthew 5:14).

So God is not shining His light in your heart to hide it there, and He's not putting it in there so men cannot see it. It's in your heart, but it's supposed to shine in the same strength, brilliance, and glory that a city built on a hill would shine.

God's Light Shines Through Words

How can we get God's internal illumination to shine through us? We must use the same method God used to release the life and the light that is in Him — by using the power of words. God *said*, "Let there be light," and there *was* light.

The devil gets nervous every time I get ready to speak. He runs around and works overtime before I've said a word. He tells people, "Don't listen to him!" He whispers in their ears, "False doctrine!" He says to someone else, "Not for you."

Why does he do this? He's afraid of what I'm going to *say*. And if that doesn't work, he messes around with the sound system. Isn't that the truth? The devil gets nervous because words are not dead; they are *alive!* They are spirit and they are life.

Someone may say, "I don't believe that. I don't have any power in my words, because God does not want to help me."

Words have just as much power to bind you as God's Word has to set you free. In the Old Testament, Moses challenged the children of Israel, "Choose life" (blessing) in Deuteronomy 30:19.

The Test of Faith

In order to choose something God is going to give you, you must believe something you haven't seen yet. That's the test of faith.

It's not a great thing for me to believe that I've got a ministry, but it is a great thing to believe that the ministry is going to go beyond what I see in the natural.

"Now faith is the substance of things hoped for, the evidence of things not seen," according to Hebrews 11:1. Faith in the now is the substance, the pink slip, the title deed. It is the tangible, visible assurance that proves to me that I already possess what I don't yet see.

That means I can begin to speak words that declare, herald, publish, and proclaim what I don't yet see in the natural. That's where your test of faith is.

Do you want to be victorious in God? Start being like Him. He didn't say, "We're *hoping* light will be," or, "Let us try our best to make man in our image." No, God *spoke* it, and it stood fast. He *proclaimed* it, and it happened!

God's Report About Your Future

God said to you and me, "Since you're made in my image and in my likeness, believe my report." Have you ever thought about it? God's report is usually set in the future. God's report is about a victory you have not yet won. God's report is about a heaven you have never visited. God's report is about a prosperity that exceeds your present circumstances. God's report is about a destiny you have not yet achieved.

When do you believe God's report? Not when it happens, but *before* it ever comes. When do you start talking it? *Before* it ever happens. That demands strength, because it means you've got to make a decision to walk and talk faith even when you don't *feel* like it.

We can experience a victory in our Christian walk that will last a lifetime, because it's not dependent upon a special manifestation or an impartation of the Spirit. It is God's power linked in with your decision that says, "I'm going to hold on to my power through words and act in accordance with the ways of God."

If we would make that decision, we would begin to conquer every area of our life where we are not victorious, and our direction will be up, up, up. Every day with Jesus would truly be sweeter than the day before.

Living in the Glory Realm

If you have a little light, it's because you're choosing to hear a little and do a little of what God says. How do I know that? The Bible says, "Be ye doers of the word, and not hearers only, deceiving your own selves" (James 1:22). James tells us to be doers of what we hear.

Psalm 119:130 says, "The entrance of thy words giveth light; it giveth understanding unto the simple." When God's Word enters my heart, it immediately enlightens my spirit man and gives me understanding.

In Second Corinthians 4:6 we read, "God...hath shined in our hearts, to give the light of the knowledge of the glory of God that shines in the face of Jesus Christ."

That word "glory" refers to the *shekinah* glory, the realm where God lives. If you tune into this dimension, you've tuned into the heavenly realm of God. When you're in that realm, anything can happen!

Positioned for a Move of God

We must learn to position ourselves for a move of God. If we position ourselves correctly, when the move of God comes, we will be prepared for it. But if it comes when we're not ready, we won't recognize it!

Throughout history, men have failed to discern when the Spirit of God was moving. Some men were right in the middle of a move of God and somehow managed to miss it every time. They were so blinded by the distractions of this world, they were not in tune with what God was saying to them.

We must allow the Word of God to move us to the point of change.

The Word of God says that God gave us this power, and the excellency of it, in earthen vessels. That tells me that when God speaks, it brings light to my heart, and it brings understanding and knowledge. When that happens, then, it brings *faith.*

Why God Speaks To Men

Faith comes by *hearing.* God doesn't just talk to talk. He talks to move men to action. We have learned to come to church and hear a sermon. Many in the church are blind and starving to death spiritually, because all they've been doing is hearing and hearing and hearing.

If all you've been doing is being a hearer of the Word, and it hasn't produced spiritual muscle and strength to lead you further in your commitment to God, you need to reevaluate the way you receive and why you are not changing. God is raising up a people who are interested in what He *says.*

Let me give you the bad news first: You'll never amount to anything unless you do it the way God has called you to do it. I'll tell you something else: You'll never defeat the devil unless you do it in God's prescribed fashion.

All He's trying to do is impart strength. All He's going to do is give you the Word. All He's going to do is tell you His report.

8

It takes strength to believe what God is saying. It takes commitment to appropriate it into our hearts. And it takes a decision that says, "I'm going to do what God says to do in His Word. I'm going to fight the good fight of faith, and I will win."

A day is coming when God's law and His Word will be the only things spoken on planet Earth. It's not here yet, but there is coming a day when God puts His kingdom on planet Earth, and Jesus Christ's Church, His Word, and His will, will rule and reign. Until then, we are engaged in a battle that is fought with words.

Jesus Speaks With Authority

The Bible says that Jesus spoke with authority: "...for with authority commandeth he even the evil spirits, and they do obey him" (Mark 1:27). Jesus had authority in His words, and He still does!

Why didn't Jesus telepathically "think the devil away"? Why didn't He just think the devil out? Because it does not matter what you *feel* in your heart, or what your intentions are, or what you think you're going to do for God some day. Unless you unleash the spirit and the power that's in you and trigger it through your words, it won't create an explosion in your life.

Someone will say, "Well, God knows that I love Him in my heart, and I'm just a heart-praiser."

Start praising Him out loud. Start giving Him glory. Unless you release the spirit and power that's in you, it won't create a spiritual explosion around you. The Bible instructs us to take "the sword of the Spirit, which is the word of God" (Ephesians 6:17).

Jesus spoke, and the devils obeyed. We recognize that the kingdom of God is *with power*, don't we, and we notice that the apostle Paul said, "And my speech and my preaching was not with enticing words of man's wisdom, but *in demonstration of the Spirit and of power*" (1 Corinthians 2:4).

Paul didn't use enticing words of man's wisdom. What kind of speech and what kind of preaching *did* Paul use? He brought forth the demonstration of the Spirit and of power.

That tells me that *God's Spirit and power are injected into the words we speak by the inspiration of the Holy Spirit.*

The Hidden Power of Your Words

That tells me that the devil is terrified of man's God-given ability to release words. *Powerful words come out of you like a missile that heads straight for its target and hits the bull's-eye in the kingdom of darkness!*

You ought to be ready to pull the trigger on every lie the devil brings against you. When the devil questions, "Hath God said?" you should reply, "The promises of God are yea and amen for him that believes," and — *boom* — trigger those words right into the heart of hell!

God gave you power. That power won't work in spite of you, and it won't work automatically. That power will only work when you use the abilities God placed within you in the beginning, in creation. The greatest of these abilities is the ability to decide direction and destiny in life. Man's freewill is the greatest gift given to him by God.

Your Destiny: Your Decision

Do you want to be miserable? Do you want to have a pity-party and be depressed, oppressed, regressed, or obsessed? Go ahead. You may. It's your privilege. God gave it to you. He put within you the ability to choose.

You can choose to be wherever you want to be. You can be the "tail" if you want to, but I'm going to be the "head" (Deuteronomy 28:13)! You can live in the outskirts, in the shallow waters, if you want to, but there are people who have plunged into the deep waters.

You can live on the hillside if you want to, but there are those who have climbed the high mountains in God. You can soar with the wings of turkeys, but there are some who have decided to soar with the wings of eagles. They are part of the generation that won't settle for partial commitment to God.

In other words, you've got a God-given right to decide how far you'll go and what direction you'll go, and even God can't violate that decision. If you want to go the right way, you must position yourself by how you think and what you speak.

Paul gave Timothy some advice about this in Second Timothy 3:15:

And that from a child thou hast known the holy scriptures, which are able to make thee wise unto salvation through faith which is in Christ Jesus.

What does that mean? Paul is telling Timothy, "Since you were a child you have known the holy scriptures, which are *able* to make you wise through faith." Paul didn't say that the Scriptures had made Timothy wise; he said they were *able* to make him wise.

Mixing the Word With Faith

That means you can hear a sermon but leave the church just as weak spiritually as when you entered. That means you can hear me, go home and debate whether or not I match up to your favorite preacher, and still be on the same level you were before.

Unless you mix what you're hearing with faith, it's almost better that you didn't hear the Word! The Bible says, "the word preached did not profit them, *not being mixed with faith* in them that heard it" (Hebrews 4:2).

The Word will bring faith with it. However, there is a way that people can receive the Word of God but not receive the faith of the Word. How? The Word will always bring a responsibility with it. People can reject that responsibility.

When God speaks to you, He gives you a responsibility. When He says, "You're my child," He's saying, "You're committed to Me." And when He says, "You're the light," He's

11

saying, "Now you're going to shine as a witness." That's a commitment.

So if we choose to receive one part of the Word and say, "Yes, I'm a light, but I'm a silent light," we're not mixing the Word with faith.

We must decide to mix what we hear with faith so we can perform it.

Chapter 2
God-Breathed Words

All scripture is given by inspiration of God, and is prof–itable for doctrine, for reproof, for correction, for instruction in righteousness:

That the man of God may be perfect, thoroughly furnished unto all good works.

2 Timothy 3:16,17

That word "Scripture" is the Greek word *gramma*. It means "letters of the alphabet" or "words." God is saying through Paul, "All the grammas of God, from the alphas all the way through the omegas, are the words of God..."

The Bible, however, is not called "the words of God"; it is called "the Word of God," because God put a message in His Bible, and that message is one word to mankind.

It is one form of word, one kind of spirit: the Spirit of God. And that message is one kind of report: a good report. It may come in the form of many words, but it's one report, and it's a good report.

The Bible says that the grammas of God — the alphas through the omegas, His alphabet, His inspired utterance, His words — are *God-breathed*.

Remember, in Genesis 1:26 we saw where God said, "Let us make man in our image," and in Genesis 2:7 the Bible says, "And the Lord God formed man of the dust of the ground, and breathed into his nostrils *the breath of life....*"

13

And in John 1:4 it says of Jesus, the Word, "In him was life; and the life was the light of men." This means the breath of life is in every word of Scripture we ever hear.

Words That Are Alive

Have you ever tried to talk while you're inhaling? Go ahead and say "hallelujah" and inhale at the same time. Words have been designed by God to carry with them breath and life.

When words come out of you, part of your humanity goes with them; the authority God gave you to operate on planet Earth goes out with those words. They're *breathed.*

As you're breathing the same words God breathed into you, both you and God are breathing through you. And when both you and God are breathing, something will happen!

All of God's words, all Scripture, is God-breathed, so there is the exhale of the Holy Spirit in the Bible. What does that mean? The words of the Bible are *alive!* They are breath. They are life. They are *zoe.* They will charge you up with the life of God!

...the letter killeth, but the spirit giveth life.

2 Corinthians 3:6

The Spirit *what?* "Giveth life." That tells me that God never sends His Word unless it is filled with part of His Spirit. As a matter of fact, His Word is alive. Just because it's printed with ink on paper does not make it dead.

Breathing What God Has Breathed

When you read God's Word with the eyes of faith, you encounter the Spirit of the Word, which is alive beyond the pages. You can fold up the Bible, but you can never fold up the King of kings and the Lord of lords. He's alive and well, and He's among His people, in His Church.

Therefore, when I put His words in my mouth and speak them, not only am I breathing out what I choose to believe in life, but I am breathing out what God has breathed, sanctioned, anointed, and sent to deliver His people. He said in Isaiah:

> **For as the rain cometh down, and the snow from heaven...so shall my word be that goeth forth out of my mouth: it shall not return unto me void, but it shall accomplish that which I please, and it shall prosper in the thing whereto I sent it.**
>
> **Isaiah 55:10,11**

You see, God breathed it, it came into the earth realm, and now His Word is alive and at work in the hearts of people, trying to get us to let go of the limits of the natural and go on a journey in God's Word into the destiny He foretold and intended for us. That destiny is Christlikeness; it's to be like Jesus.

Life for the Spirit Man

Jesus told Satan, "Man shall not live by bread alone, but by every word that proceedeth out of the mouth of God" (Matthew 4:4). We find in this verse that the words that proceed out of God's mouth carry life, and they can cause your spirit man to live!

When you hear God's words, your spirit man can be charged and can live by the strength of the words that proceed out of the mouth of God.

That word "God-breathed," which is interpreted as "inspiration" in Second Timothy 3:16, is the word *theonustos*. *Theo* means God, and *nustos* comes from the word *pneuma*, which is "breath" or "spirit." So every word God speaks is literally breathed by God!

The Scripture goes on to say that when you mix God's words with faith (Hebrews 4:2), you'll receive the life and breath of God into your life. And when you do, you can become a man or a woman of God who is perfect and "thoroughly furnished unto *all* good works."

That word "thoroughly" is the word *exarteso*, "to furnish" or "to equip fully." When the Word accomplishes full equipping in you, you will do the works of Christ.

Christ's Presence in the Word

This is where we've been missing it. We've been hearing the Word of God, but failing to receive the breath, life, energy, force, character, and entity of Jesus Christ — *His personal presence in the Word.*

If you fail to receive that with the message you're hearing, you will fail to receive the ability to do His works in that moment in time.

What are His works? Raising the dead, healing the sick, casting out devils, cleansing the lepers, unstopping deaf ears, opening blinded eyes, turning sinners to God, cursing the fig trees, moving the mountains, walking on water — these are His works.

Unless we receive the breath, the life, and the Spirit in what He says, we won't be transformed into His image and be able to do His works.

So one thing we need to do is not only hear what God is saying, but hear it *in our spirit man*, mix it with faith, and let it live.

Ask What You Will

Jesus said this in John 15:7, and I've paraphrased it for modern readers as follows: "If you live in my word, and my word lives in you — not on the shelf, not in the study, not in the tape deck, not at the church, not in your wife, nor in your husband — you may ask whatever you will, and it shall be done for you."

In other words, *if you position yourself to fit the criteria of God, He can never deny the answer to what you pray for.*

Don't tell anyone, "God is choosing not to answer me." That simply reveals the fact that the Word is not yet living in you. Why? Because if we position ourselves according to

16

Jesus, and His Word lives in us, we will ask what we will and it *shall* be done for us. He didn't say "maybe," He didn't say "sometimes," and He didn't say it "could." He said it *"shall"* be done.

God Wants To Make You an Alien!

You see, God is trying to make you an alien, and you won't let Him! If the Church of today would let God have His way, we'd scare the world to the altar!

The world would start to see people who have fire in their eyes, a glow about them, miracles in their hands, and a positive report in their mouth. They'd see people who are water-walkers, mountain-movers, dead men-raisers, miracle-workers; people who are full of "joy unspeakable and full of glory."

The Bible says, "The people that do know their God shall be strong, and do exploits" (Daniel 11:32). How do we know our God? By knowing how He talks, what He says, and what He wants. We let His Word do in us what He sent it to do.

Do you know what God sent His Word to do in you? To produce the life of our resurrected Lord and Master, for anything short of the life of the resurrected Lord and Master is putting limits on God.

That tells me that we ought to start changing right now, because His Word didn't come to tantalize our intellect; it came to change us. And God said, "I'm not taking that Word back. It is not going to return unto Me void."

Do you know what the word "void" means? It means "empty." So God is saying, "My Word is not returning empty!"

So God spoke His Word regarding you and me, and His Word has come into our lives. It will not leave us alone. It will continue to inspire, correct, reprove, and rebuke us until we say yes to the Word of God and take the limits off God.

Then, suddenly, God's Word will begin to actively produce in us Christ who is alive and well in His Church. When this happens, the world will see a people who have let go of the limits of the natural and have stepped into God's realm of divine manifestation!

The Word is *not* going to return void. It *is* going to produce in us what God sent it to produce.

God's Word Brings Understanding

Now look at Hebrews 11:3: "Through faith we understand...." Remember, the Word of God brings *light*, it gives *understanding*, and God shined in our hearts to give us "the light of the *knowledge* of the glory of God in the face of Jesus Christ."

Someone will say, "Well, you never know what God is going to do."

You ought to walk in the light, then, because when we walk in the light as Jesus is the light, we have fellowship or understanding one with another (1 John 1:7). In John 15:15, Jesus said, "I no longer call you servants, because a servant doesn't know what his master is doing. I call you friends, because I'm going to tell you what I'm doing." You *can* know what God is going to do!

If you never know what God is doing, change roads and get in the light so His Word can bring you understanding. How can you understand God's ways? You can only understand through faith.

That means you have to *believe* you understand before you ever understand. And that means that you have to believe that God directs you before He ever directs you, because you receive from God through faith.

Some will say, "God never tells me what to do. I wish He'd tell me what to do."

That's right, and He won't tell you, either, because in order for God to direct you, He's got to get your report, or what you believe, on the subject. If you tell Him, "I believe You don't direct me," God will say, "I second that."

People come up to me all the time after I preach and teach, and say, "Prophet, I need a word. Pray for me for direction." They want me to prophesy over them what they ought to do.

But the Bible says, "The steps of a righteous man are ordered of the Lord" (Psalm 37:23). That means, if I want to be directed of the Lord, I've got to believe first that I'm the righteousness of God in Christ Jesus. And if I am, and if God is no respecter of persons, I will have direction, whether or not I see it yet.

Therefore, when the devil comes to you and says, "You don't have any direction!" just tell him, "Devil, I don't *need* any direction to whip you! I'm going to win, standing right where I'm at."

From Invisible to Visible

How were the natural, tangible things created? I'm referring to the universe, the stars, and the earth itself — mankind, animals, angels. How were they created? The Bible says:

Through faith we understand that the worlds were framed by the word of God, so that things which are seen were not made of things which do appear.

Hebrews 11:3

And that means they were made by the Word of God, or by the words that God spoke.

Some will argue, "Well, get out of the Bible. Get out of that thing about hearing God and talking about what God says. That's all fine and good, but get down to earth."

Earth was created because God spoke, and Jesus said that mountains would be moved because a man will speak to them: "...whosoever shall say to this mountain..." (Mark 11:23).

19

Why Do You Face Obstacles?

Do you know why mountains are here? So Christians can move them. That's right. Why do you run into obstacles? Because you're more than a conqueror. Why is there an enemy? Because he's going to become God's footstool.

The devil is here to be walked on by the Church, bound up by believers, and cast out by Holy Ghost folks. It puts a little fun into this spiritual race knowing that.

The other day, someone said to me, "Well, I tried to do what you said. I told the devil to get off my back, but he wouldn't listen."

Of course, he's not going to listen. Do you think he wants to give up being carried around on a Christian's back? I'd rather be carried by a Christian than by anyone else, and so would the devil. But God never said, "Carry the devil on your back, and then tell him to get off." God said, "Walk on him!"

Like the man told me, "Brother, just keep on doing what you're doing, and God will keep on anointing you." He added, "Remember, like Oral Roberts said, 'Greater is He that's in you than he that is in the world.'"

Only Scripture Is Effective

How many of you know that Oral Roberts did *not* come up with that statement? He didn't originate "Greater is He that is in you than he that is in the world." It's a Bible verse from First John 4:4.

It will never work for me if Oral Roberts said it; however, it *will* work for me if God showed it to Oral Roberts, and he repeated it, and it is the immovable, unshakable, eternal Word of God. Then I can count on it, for it *is* true, as the actual verse reads, that "...greater is he that is in you, than he that is in the world."

Why? Because God said it, and His words are life and truth; and through faith I can understand their reality. On the other hand, if I believe something that came to me second-hand — something created through a preacher's fleshly devising — how am I going to be able to use that against the devil? It's not Scripture, and it won't work.

God's Words Hold the Universe Together

The Bible says, "Who being the brightness of His glory," speaking of Jesus, "and the express image of his person, and upholding all things by the word of his power..." (Hebrews 1:3).

Did you know the whole universe is still glued together? Gravity is still working, and the balance of the universe is still active, because everything is glued by invisible, God-breathed words that He spoke I don't know how many zillions of years ago.

If you could kill God's Word, you could blow up the universe — but, of course, you can't kill God's Word.

The Bible says that God magnified His Word above His name (Psalm 138:2). His Word is in a realm of its own. It's alive, it operates in you and me, and it brings divine change.

We become carriers of explosive power, because we are carriers of words that give glory to the King of kings and the Lord of lords. *These words are going to blow up the devil!*

Pay Attention to God

My son, attend to my words; incline thine ear unto my sayings.

Let them not depart from thine eyes; keep them in the midst of thine heart.

For they are life unto those that find them, and health to all their flesh.

Proverbs 4:20-22

Notice what God is saying to us: "Attend to my words." Pay attention to them. "Incline your ear to them." Hear them. "Let them not depart from your eyes." Look at the promises of God. "Keep them in the midst of your heart." Hide them in your spirit man.

Why is God saying that we should do all these things? Because it's important for our triumph in the earth realm. It's imperative that we embrace the life that is in God's Word. If we do, we'll be founded on a strong foundation, and the Bible says that the devil will have no place in us (John 14:30; Ephesians 4:27).

Sinning Against God

Look again at the phrase, "keep them in the midst of thine heart." Remember, the Bible says, "Thy word have I hid in mine heart, that I might not sin against thee" (Psalm 119:11). Why? Because His Word is *alive* in our heart.

Now let me explain something to you. When we think of sinning against God, we automatically think of breaking the Ten Commandments, or we think of a sin like theft, murder, adultery, backbiting, hatred, variance, or whatever.

But God said if we will hide His Word in our hearts, we won't sin against Him. Why? Because anything that's a violation of what God said is sinning against God.

We also read where the Bible said that God's words are life and health to all your flesh (Proverbs 4:22). Some people complain, "I always get sick. I'm just sickly, and I don't understand it. I wish God would heal me."

That's sinning against God, because if the Word was hid in my heart, when I open my mouth, the confession that's going to come out of my mouth is, "By His stripes I was healed" (1 Peter 2:24).

It doesn't matter how I feel; I'm not going to sin against God. So if I feel weak, I'm not going to run around saying, "I'm so weak." Instead, I'm going to say, "As my days are, so shall my strength be" (Deuteronomy 33:25), because that's what God's Word in my heart is.

Some of us have been hiding the wrong word in our heart, like, "The thing which I greatly feared has come upon me" (Job 3:25). That's the wrong word!

Rightly Dividing the Word of Truth

Instead, we need to hide words in our hearts that proven men and women of God speak by the inspiration of the Holy Spirit, because the Bible says, "Study to shew thyself approved unto God, a workman that needeth not to be ashamed, rightly dividing the word of truth" (2 Timothy 2:15).

We need to divide what the devil and the flesh said from what God said. Don't quote the devil; quote God. Don't quote the flesh; quote God.

There are many things in the Bible that were truly said, and they are *a* truth, but they are not *the* truth. *A truth* will not set you free. Jesus said, "Ye shall know *the truth*, and the truth shall make you free" (John 8:32). Not *a* truth.

You say, "Well, I don't want to lie, so when I have a headache, I'm going to *say* I have a headache."

How many have ever thought that? Yes, it is *a* fact that you are having a headache, but *the* truth says, "By His stripes you were healed." What are you going to believe — *a* truth, or *the* truth?

You say, "Well, I'm having wrong thoughts and feelings. They don't resemble Jesus, they don't resemble the fruit of the Spirit, and I'm not going to lie about having them."

That is *a* fact: You are having wrong thoughts, and you are feeling things that don't resemble the fruit of the Spirit; but *the* truth is, you're the righteousness of God in Christ Jesus, and the truth is, you *have* the mind of Christ (Philippians 2:5).

You may say, "I'm confused."

That is *a* fact. You may be experiencing the natural symptoms of confusion, but your spiritual position in God is, God is not the author of confusion (1 Corinthians 14:33). And the truth in God is, "Thou wilt keep him in perfect peace, whose mind is stayed on thee..." (Isaiah 26:3).

Walk Above Your Difficulties

So, instead of saying what you feel in the natural, you ought to say what you believe by faith. When you grasp that truth, you'll walk above and not beneath your difficulties.

Jesus told the Father, "Father, I thank thee that thou hast heard me. And I know that thou hearest me always..." (John 11:41,42). But when we ask Christians, "Does God always hear you?" they mumble, "Well, I *hope* so."

Jesus said that if we ask anything in His name, He hears us. That's what Jesus said. I didn't say it.

"Well, brother, I don't want to lie and say God always hears me when He *doesn't.*"

"Well, why doesn't He?"

"I don't know."

I'll tell you why. It's because you're saying He doesn't. You're choosing to believe past history — how it's been for you in your life until now — instead of doing what the apostle Paul said:

...this one thing I do, forgetting those things which are behind, and reaching forth unto those things which are before,

I press toward the mark for the prize of the high calling of God in Christ Jesus.

Philippians 3:13,14

Finding and Speaking God's Word

So I'm going to hide God's Word in my heart, and I'm going to speak it. When I do, God's Word is going to go to work. The Lord said if I put His Word in my heart, keep it before my eyes, attend to it, and incline my ears to it, it would be life to those that find it and health to all their flesh.

Notice, however, that I've got to *find* the words before they become life and health to me. I thought it was easy to find God's Word. I thought you just opened the Bible and found it, but that's not so.

You can open the Bible and read it, but that doesn't mean you've found God's Word. You can come to church and hear it, but that doesn't mean you've found it. You can even memorize it and quote it, but that doesn't mean you've found God's Word.

You ask, ""How do I know when I've found it?"

Don't worry. When you find it, you'll know. It won't matter to you then what happens; you will have the assurance that God's will is going to be done in your life.

This is what happens when you find God's Word: As you hear it, that Word ceases to be simply a lesson or a message you are exposed to. Once you receive it in your heart and allow its unlimited expression, it becomes alive and expresses itself through you!

So when you receive God's Word, you'll know it! You knew it when you received God's Word concerning salvation, didn't you? You knew that you knew that you knew that when you said the sinner's prayer, you were going to get saved, didn't you?

You didn't come to the altar and say, "I *hope* God hears me when I say the sinner's prayer." No, you were thoroughly convinced that you had found His Word about salvation, and you knew that all you had to do was believe in your heart and confess with your mouth, and you would be saved.

Who guaranteed that this would happen? You found God's Word. The Bible says that God's words are "life unto those that find them, and health to all their flesh." The Bible says, "Keep thy heart with all diligence; for out of it are the issues of life" (Proverbs 4:23).

Guard Your Heart

Guard your heart with strong diligence and commitment. Don't allow foreign elements, such as lies or spiritual influences of the enemy, to trouble your heart. Guard it from the words and the thoughts of the devil, because God intends it to be a vessel of honor.

God intends that the issues of life should pour out of your heart. How are the issues of life expressed through you? *Through words.* Out of your heart the issues of life are expressed.

If I spoke ten thousand words in tongues, it might bless you, and it would bless me — but tongues can't express the issues of life.

Jesus said, "He that believeth on me, as the scripture hath said, out of his belly shall flow rivers of living water" (John 7:38).

The words of God are going to begin to pour forth out of God's people. These words will resemble missiles, darts, and weapons of war. They will hit things in the Spirit. They will hit the adversary!

The devil is going to try to shoot a fiery dart at you, but God said you can quench *all* his fiery darts! Take up the sword of the Spirit and slash the enemy, because the truth sets God's people free.

A Prayer

"Father, I thank You for your words and for your perfect will for my life. I choose to receive and believe your words, and to mix them with faith. I believe now in what You've done, but I also believe in what You're going to do.

"I thank You for my journey, my victory, my promotion, my healing, and my prosperity. I thank You for the mind of Christ, the words of God, clear direction, steadfastness, stability, strength, clarity, and wisdom. I thank You for the fruit of the Spirit, the gifts of the Holy Spirit, the armor of God, the Name of Jesus, and the blood of the Lamb.

"I thank You that I'm the winner, and that I can do all things through Christ which strengthens me, which means I can do all things through your living Word.

"Lord, speak, and as You speak, I'll be changed. Your Word will not fall on deaf ears, on dry land, or on parched land, but it will

fall on good soil, and it will be lodged deep in my heart. I'll hide it, and I won't sin against You.

"I'll speak the report of the Lord, and believe that I'll possess my land of promise. There is no giant big enough to stop me. There is no devil, no battle, no mountain, no challenge, no obstacle, no hardship, no limit that will hold me back. I am going all the way, for greater is He that is in me than he that is in the world. Amen."

Chapter 3
Words As Weapons

When mankind speaks, whether on behalf of God or on behalf of the devil, those words pack power.

Why? Because God has invested authority, power, and ability in *words*. Ever since God breathed into man the breath of life, man received authority and power that could be released through him in the form of words.

Even the unregenerate, unsaved individual who is not Spirit filled has within his soulish makeup, just because he is human, a certain amount of power. You can see this in the New Age Movement, in the cults, and in satanism with its curses.

When you visit African nations, you find that they take curses very seriously. They know that people can speak words that are charged with human, soulish power and then are infused with demonic force — and that is known as witchcraft.

On the other hand, God chose to redeem a people who will accept redemption, to deliver a people who will accept deliverance, and Jesus promised, "I'm going to fill you with power, after that the Holy Ghost is come upon you" (Acts 1:8). That power He gave us is expressed and released when we speak the report of the Lord.

We can believe it, meditate on it, keep it before our eyes, hide it in our heart, and then speak it; and those words will come out of our being as weapons of battle that will slay the enemy as well as shape our circumstances and allow them to line up with God's will and purpose.

Justified by Your Words

Jesus said in Matthew 12:37, "For by thy words thou shalt be justified, and by thy words thou shall be condemned." Justification is not an automatic condition that operates in spite of your decisions.

In other words, I can't decide to be condemned and be justified. I can't decide to be defeated and be justified. I can't decide to be a castaway and be justified.

I can't approach the throne of God and say, "God, I know You've never heard me before, and chances are, You're not going to hear me again," and be justified. It doesn't work automatically.

I have to be justified the way Jesus said: *by words.* He didn't say by your spouse's words or your pastor's words. He said, "By *thy* words thou shalt be justified, and by *thy* words thou shalt be condemned."

That tells me that the Lord left the final decision to us. For example, God told the children of Israel, "I call heaven and earth to record this day against you, that I have set before you life and death, blessing and cursing: therefore choose life..." (Deuteronomy 30:19).

We should be like Joshua, who said, "As for me and my house, we shall serve the Lord." How many see power in those words?

"Well, Joshua, how do you *know* you're going to serve the Lord? What if you backslide?"

We, like Joshua, can answer that we're not of those who draw back; we're of those who believe, to the saving of our souls. How do we know? Because that's the way it is; that's what we decided.

Our words can become a justifying, redeeming, delivering factor in our mouth that enables us to walk a life of constant transformation before God.

A Big Problem: A Big Mouth

Many people, however, have a big problem they cannot overcome, and that problem is their big mouth. The reason it's a big problem is, instead of yielding it to a big God, they yield it to a little devil.

They're always speaking negatively, stating how hard everything is, and their words snare them. The Bible says, "Thou art snared with the words of thy mouth, thou art taken with the words of thy mouth" (Proverbs 6:2).

The Bible says, "...the mouth of the upright shall deliver them" (Proverbs 12:6), and, "...the tongue of the wise is health" (Proverbs 12:18). Why? Because such people yield their members — in this case, their tongues — as instruments of righteousness to God.

If Jesus taught that what I say will either justify or condemn me, I'm going to say what justifies me.

When Tongues Rise Up Against You

Isaiah 54:17 says, "No weapon that is formed against thee shall prosper; and every tongue that shall rise against thee in judgment thou shalt condemn. This is the heritage of the servants of the Lord, and their righteousness is of me, saith the Lord."

Listen to what God just said: "It does not matter what kind of weapon the devil forms against you. It does not matter how strong that weapon looks. As a matter of fact, it does not matter what kind of tongue rises up against you."

That tells me that the Lord associates demonic weapons with words. That tells me that God is saying, "What the devil uses as weapons are curses and words he speaks against God's law and God's plan for your life."

The Devil's Diagnosis

Let me give you an example. A believer starts to get symptoms in her body. She feels pain, she feels weak, and she starts having negative thoughts that say, "You shall die and not live." (That's a weapon the devil launched.)

This sister then goes to some educated man who specializes in guesswork, and he also tells her, "You shall die and not live."

A woman like this came to one of my meetings in the Midwest. She had to be carried up to the altar by several men. She had a bowel disease that had paralyzed her lower extremities. She couldn't walk, and she was in excruciating pain.

I asked, "What's wrong?"

She told me, and I asked, "What did your doctors say?"

"It's incurable," she replied.

Heaven's Diagnosis

How many know that was a tongue that rose up against her? How many know that was a weapon that the devil formed against her?

I said to the congregation, "How many of you want to hear *heaven's diagnosis*? It is, 'By His stripes you *were* healed!'" When I laid hands on her, she shot off like she'd been shot out of a cannon.

I said, "Run!" She started running all over that church — healed instantly by the power of God, for "no weapon formed against you shall prosper."

The Lord is raising up people who refuse to repeat, broker, carry, or deliver messages He didn't send. They refuse to carry their own opinions, the devil's plans, their skeptical friends' opinions, or anything else that God didn't send.

They will only carry the Word of the Lord, and they choose to condemn every tongue that rises against them — because their righteousness is of God.

Why can't the devil condemn them? Because your own words will either justify you or condemn you.

"Return to Sender"

If the devil can't get your tongue to work for him, he can't get his "packages" — his destructive weapons, his fiery darts — delivered to you.

After a while, he gets the package back. On it you've written, "Cancer—Return to Sender!" You didn't cooperate.

So when you start to feel a symptom, don't say, "I'm catching the Hong Kong flu. I'm under the weather. I'm coming down with something."

It's ridiculous for someone to say, "I'm coming down with something" when they don't even know what it is, yet they believe it. The devil will accommodate them. He'll say, "Yes, we have any number of things here for you to come down with. Which do you prefer?" He's like the announcer who comes on television and says, "Do you have hay fever? Would you like to?"

If we would not yield our lips, our tongue, our words, or our thought life to what the devil wants us to speak, we would be justified by what we speak on behalf of God.

The Devil's Subtle Attacks

That's why, when a tongue rises against you, you can condemn it. The tongue is not rising against you and telling you an obvious message of contradiction; it's coming to you in a thought form that says, "You're sure tired, and your body is acting a little strange. You should have that checked."

The devil will come to you and say, "You know, it doesn't look like your finances are shaping up, and it doesn't look like there is any way out in the natural."

He will come to you and say, "God must not be pleased with where you are; that's why you're in the situation you're in."

That tongue is not going to come against you in a visible, clearly discernable way. It's going to be subtle about what it says to you. The only way you can condemn that tongue and resist that weapon is by justifying yourself in the sight of God *through what you choose to put in your mouth.*

When Attacks Come

When symptoms come, I say, "By His stripes I was healed." When the devil comes against me through financial lack, I quote Philippians 4:19: "My God shall supply all of my need according to His riches in glory by Christ Jesus."

When I seem to be facing a great battle, I claim First John 4:4: "Greater is He that is in me than he that is in the world." In this way, I justify myself in the sight of God by putting His word to work in my life, rather than by putting the word of the devil to work in my life.

Both sources carry power. The devil's power is borrowed and stolen. God's power, through Jesus Christ, was gained in conquest.

When Jesus came into the earth as a man anointed by the Holy Spirit, He defeated the devil. After His crucifixion, He went down into the lower parts of the earth, and He didn't come up again empty-handed!

The Bible says, "And having spoiled principalities and powers, he made a show of them openly, triumphing over them in it" (Colossians 2:15). He rose again with the keys of death, hell, and the grave, and said, "All power is given unto me in heaven and in earth" (Matthew 28:18).

Power Over the Enemy!

Then He said, "Behold, I give unto *you* power to tread on serpents and scorpions, and over all the power of the enemy, and nothing shall by any means hurt *you*" (Luke 10:19).

Let's go back to the promise in Isaiah 54: "No weapon that is formed against *you* shall prosper." Why isn't it going to hurt you? *Because you're not giving it your tongue.*

What if the apostle Paul, right after the snake bit him, had complained, "My God, I survived that shipwreck, but now I'm going to die of snake bite!" How many know he would have dropped dead?

But Paul shook the snake back into the fire. He gave no place to the devil. And that's the kind of people God is raising up — a people who won't give the devil a place in their life.

Don't let the devil talk out of your mouth. Some people say, "Well, I'm just not adequate. I'm so weak. I don't have any wisdom. I don't have your kind of faith. God knows how I am; He made me like this."

No, He didn't! And He's working overtime to try to change you. But every time you come to church and the Word of God cleanses and justifies you, and you shout, "Hallelujah," and then you walk outside and hit a battle, you immediately start binding and snaring yourself by *what you say.*

Redeemed From the Curse

Galatians 3:13,14 says:

Christ hath redeemed us from the curse of the law, being made a curse for us: for it is written, Cursed is every one that hangeth on a tree:

That the blessing of Abraham might come on the Gentiles through Jesus Christ; that we might receive the promise of the Spirit through faith.

We've heard teaching that amplified and emphasized what the curse of the law is, haven't we? We realize that the curse of the law is death, poverty, sickness, and falling short of the glory of God.

But here I want to show you a curse that Paul likened to carrying a dead body on your back. He said in Romans 7:24, "O wretched man that I am! who shall deliver me from the body of this death?"

Here Paul described what it was like to try to be righteous, but to fall short of it; to ever attempt, but never achieve; to ever strive, but never reach the goal. You see, the Old Testament proved one thing: "All have sinned, and come short of the glory of God." It proved that all our righteousness is as filthy rags.

God established this law, which was a righteous and perfect law; a law that said, "If you perform this law fully, you will reap the rewards of being what the Lord declared was righteous." Yet not one person on planet Earth could perform this law fully, because "All have sinned, and come short of the glory of God" (Romans 3:23).

The law said, "He that doeth them must live by them." In other words, you don't start the race of life as righteous; however, if by chance you should keep every jot and tittle of the law and finish the race without breaking one commandment, you're pronounced righteous.

The Worst Curse

The problem was: No one ever finished the race of life without breaking a commandment. That's the curse, and that's the worst curse you could have: the curse of ever needing a Deliverer! However, in Galatians 3:13,14, the Bible says that Jesus Christ has redeemed us from that curse!

The only One who kept the totality of the law was the One who spoke the law into existence in the first place — Jesus Christ — and no one can reach God without going through Christ.

Every word that God spoke in the law was designed to be a blessing, but it turned out to be a curse. Why? Because if you couldn't keep it, it couldn't bless you. If you couldn't perform it, it couldn't make you righteous. If you couldn't fulfill all of it, it couldn't guarantee God's blessings and abundance in your life.

Living on Credit

Therefore, each of the Old Testament saints lived on "credit," looking forward to the coming Deliverer who would deliver them and change their hearts so they would then be clean from the inside out, instead of attempting to clean themselves up from the outside in.

Here in Galatians, God says that He has redeemed us from that curse through Jesus' death on the cross. Jesus was made a curse for us, "for it is written, Cursed is every one that hangeth on a tree" (Galatians 3:13).

Why did Jesus redeem us from the curse? So the blessings of Abraham could be ours. Notice, however, that Jesus is not *going to* redeem you from the curse someday in the sweet bye-and-bye. Christ *hath* — past tense — delivered us from the curse of the law. That means we don't have to live under a curse; we can live under a blessing!

And what is a curse? It's a word, a tongue, a message, a report that *condemns*.

Living Under the Blessing

What is a blessing? It's a word, a tongue, a message, a report that *justifies*. When it justifies, it can bring all the resources God has and give them to you freely and liberally. Why? You're justified. God couldn't bypass you if He tried! *You're a perfect candidate for answered prayer.* You're a perfect candidate for His promises to be made real in your life.

No one is in a better condition to be healed than you. No one is in a better condition to be wealthy and blessed than you. No one! But you've got to allow God's Word to appropriate the blessings of Abraham for your life.

Watch how it happens: "...that we might receive the promise of the Spirit *through faith*" (Galatians 3:14). When the Spirit comes, I receive Him by faith, and then He begins to inspire me with the Word of God. I've got to use that faith to speak God's Word into my life, because by my words I am justified.

Some have said, "I'm just a sinner. I have a problem with lust. My problem is my flesh — I can't keep my flesh under."

Show me a person who talks like that, and I'll show you a person who's got a problem with lust. Show me a person who talks about depression all the time, and I'll show you a depressed person. Why? Because *by their words they are condemned.* They're pronouncing a condemnation on themselves rather than a blessing.

Frustration to Freedom

Paul was yanking his hair out in frustration under the Old Testament Dispensation when he declared in Romans 7:24, "O wretched man that I am! who shall deliver me from the body of this death?" But then in Romans 8:1 he says, "There is therefore now no condemnation to them which are in Christ Jesus, who walk not after the flesh, but after the Spirit."

Why is there no condemnation for them? Because they can keep their mouth — and with their words they are not condemned; they are justified.

They believe that Christ has destroyed the curse, so the curse cannot operate on believers who have chosen to put the Word of God in their heart and life.

The Bible says, "There shall no evil befall thee, neither shall any plague come nigh thy dwelling" (Psalm 91:10). When a plague is going around looking for a candidate to devour, and it sees a Bible-believing child of God who chooses to put the Word of God in his mouth, the plague says, "We'd better not try to go near that house!" The plague knows what is going to happen: The believer is going to rise up and say, "No, I choose blessing!"

When you operate in that realm, the whole earth can be in drought, but it will rain in your back yard. The whole earth can be in famine, but your apple tree will bear. A little boy can say, "All I've got are a couple of fishes," but you'll multiply them.

The Double-Minded Man

That's the kind of new breed God is raising up; not weak people who are tossed about with every wind of doctrine. Such people are double minded. They're blessed on Sunday morning but down and out by Monday night. As James wrote:

> **Let not that man think that he shall receive any thing of the Lord.**
>
> **A double minded man is unstable in all his ways.**
>
> **James 1:7,8**

Double mindedness manifests with a double testimony. Do you know what a double tongue is? A serpent.

The words we speak with our mouth are powerful. The reason our ministry is where it is today is because we believed what God said about it, and we put that in our mouth and refused to embrace any report that was contrary to God's perfect plan for us.

Chapter 4
The Perfect Man

My brethren, be not many masters, knowing that we shall receive the greater condemnation.

For in many things we offend all. If any man offend not in word, the same is a perfect man, and able also to bridle the whole body.

Behold, we put bits in the horses' mouths, that they may obey us; and we turn about their whole body.

James 3:1-3

Consider what James just said. He said, "In many things we offend. But if a man could manage *not* to offend in word, that man is a perfect man, and that man is a mature man who is able to bridle the whole body."

What is an offense to God? Quoting anything He didn't say. This means that some preachers' sermons are an offense to God! God didn't give them the outline, let alone the sermon.

For example, they get up and say, "Well, So-and-so got healed of cancer, but God took him with a heart attack." That's an offense to God.

But God said if we could manage not to offend in what we say, we are mature and perfect in His sight. Not only that, but we are able to bridle our whole body.

A Rebellious "House"?

Most Christians live their whole life trying to bridle their body. They think they live in a monstrous, rebellious, ready-

41

to-sin, ready-to-step-out-of-line "house" that can't stand the presence of God.

And they think that "bridling your body" means that when you want to sin, you just don't do it. You control your mind, pray in tongues, and work overtime to try to live for God.

But how many of you know that you don't bridle the horse because he's a *bad* animal; you bridle the horse because he's a *good* animal.

You bridle him because you're going to ride him. He's going to cooperate with you and take you wherever you want to go. Thus, you don't bridle him to cripple him; you bridle him to direct him, so he will carry you where you intend to go.

"Good Horsey!"

God said if you would put His Word in your mouth, you'd stop having a spirited body that bucks and kicks every time God tries to get it to go somewhere. If you'd put His Word in your mouth regarding yourself, your body would be a "good horsey" that would take you where God is leading you.

You don't want to ride a horse that you've got to beat over the head and fight to rein him left or right, to stop, and to back up. No, you want to ride a horse that responds to a loose rein, because once that horse and you become friends, you can work together.

That's what God said about your body. He said, "If you put the right word in your mouth, your body won't have a problem laying hands on the sick. Your body won't have a problem believing in Jesus, serving Him, and standing against the wiles of the devil."

When Thoughts Become Words

Your problem, however, has not been your body; it has been your tongue! Your problem results from the wrong influence invading your mind in the form of thoughts, and in you. making the wrong decision to put them in your mouth.

The Bible says, "What comes out of the heart of a man defiles a man," so the body becomes defiled.

You say, "We're going to pray for the sick over here," and your body says, "But I just don't feel like it." You say, "Well, I'm going to read the Word tonight," and your body does not want to cooperate. Instead, it snores! Why? Because you've been feeding it the wrong report.

To achieve your destiny in God, you must put God's Word in your mouth.

When the Tongue Defiles

James continues his teaching in James 3:6:

And the tongue is a fire, a world of iniquity; so is the tongue among our members, that it defileth the whole body, and setteth on fire the course of nature; and it is set on fire of hell.

Look at what the Holy Spirit has chosen to reveal to us here: The tongue can be a world of iniquity, and it can defile the whole body by what we say. So if speaking *offenses* will *defile* your body, speaking *truth* will *justify* you.

The verse goes on to say that the tongue will set on fire "the course of nature," which means the cycle of life. This explains why some of you are running into problems you prophesied on yourself in the past.

People walk around in the desert, never entering into the Promised Land, because they've chosen to speak the wrong words. They are always predicting what might go wrong.

Do you do this? Do you say, "I wonder what will go wrong next?" Are you always talking about the devil, saying, "The devil is coming against me real strong. You've got to pray for me!" That word will set on fire the course of nature, and you'll find your life being consumed with the fire of your own making!

Controlling the Tongue

In this third chapter of James, the tongue is likened to the bit we put in horses' mouths, to the helms that guide ships, and to the little fires that kindle and become great fires. Let's examine these three things.

First of all, a large ship is tossed by winds and buffeted by storms. Nevertheless, it doesn't matter how strong the wind is, or how fierce the storm; if you know how to use the rudder, you can steer that ship in the right direction, to safety.

God is saying, "Learn to use this helm." Why? So the ship of your life will go upstream. You don't want to go downstream; you want to go upstream.

Let me ask you this question: In case of a shipwreck, would you rather be left holding onto the helm, or holding onto the ship? Your choice should be to hold onto the ship, because it is more important.

The same thing applies to our body and our life. God is only interested in our words because He wants to direct our life in the right course.

We've got it turned around: We think it's a formula. We think we've got to make sure we speak something a hundred times or a thousand times before it ever happens, but that's not what God is saying.

He's saying, "I've called you. I've chosen you. And now you're already saved, already delivered, and already my righteousness. But in order for you to go where I'm sending you, you've got to use the bit; you've got to use the rudder; you've got to use your tongue the right way."

The Poisonous Tongue

We read that the tongue can set on fire the course of nature. James writes further in verses 7 and 8:

For every kind of beasts, and of birds, and of serpents, and of things in the sea, is tamed, and has been tamed of mankind:

44

But the tongue can no man tame; it is an unruly evil, full of deadly poison.

Do you realize that if the tongue is full of poison, it's only full of poison when you're speaking words of poison? It's only full of poison when you're speaking a word *other than the Word of God.*

But when you're speaking the Word and the report of the Word, it's not so, because the Holy Spirit will inspire and use your mouth to glorify Him.

Now look what happens in verse 9:

Therewith bless we God, even the Father; and therewith curse we men, which are made after the similitude of God.

Let me show you what a curse is. When Jesus walked to the barren fig tree, He didn't say, "I curse you, fig tree." No, He said, "No man eat fruit of thee hereafter for ever" (Mark 11:14). In other words, He simply made a statement appropriating the faith of God.

The next day, Peter exclaimed, "Look how quickly the fig tree you cursed has withered!" The men of Bible days knew what a curse was. *A curse was an aggressive negative declaration that proclaimed what would be.*

We who are living under the New Testament dispensation don't curse men. In other words, we don't speak negatively against men; we speak negatively only against the devil.

Appropriating the Faith of God

Why? Because the spirit of pain can be told, "You're not going to torment me anymore." The spirit of suicide can be told, "Get out of this house, and never come here again." The spirit of insanity can be told, "You have run in this family before, but you will not run in this family anymore."

God has given us the ability to speak bold statements of faith that will carry out His power through words.

When Peter commented, "Look how quickly the tree you cursed has withered," Jesus responded:

Have faith in God.

For verily I say unto you, That whosoever shall say to this mountain, Be thou removed, and be thou cast into the sea; and shall not doubt in his heart, but shall believe that those things which he saith shall come to pass [or believe in his own words]**, he shall have whatsoever he saith.**

Mark 11:22,23

Facing Your Mountain

God wants you to do something about the "mountain" you face in your life. What if a man stands in front of the mountain he faces and says, "I'm about to talk to the mountain any minute now, and when I do, watch it move. But, boy, it's a *big* mountain. Look at how big this mountain is! This mountain is so big, when it moves it's going to make a big show. Come to think of it, this mountain is so big, it's never been moved before..."

What if he begins to meditate on how big his mountain is? If he does, he'll end up with a different message in his mouth: "This mountain is so big, we've got to go around it. In fact, we'll need angels to carry us over it!"

People like this magnify their own mountain, or problem, with their own words. Something can start out as a little pebble, but before you've finished talking about it, there's nothing else in your life but that big mountain. You've magnified it with your own words.

The Bible says you can cause the tongue to be full of deadly poison when you speak the wrong words with it. You can bless the Father with it, or you can curse men which are made in the likeness of God with it. Remember, a curse is an aggressive statement which should only be used against the devil or circumstances, not men.

A Hidden Curse

Unfortunately, you don't have to say, "I curse you" to curse a person; you can simply say, "Watch her — she'll make

46

the same mistakes again. She always blows it, and she'll blow it again. Watch him — he's trying to do something for God, but he'll never prosper. He's going under." We don't even realize what we're doing when we say things like this.

Then we go and rally support against these people we've cursed by saying, "Sister, I'm just telling you this because I want you to help me pray for So-and-so. She's having struggles."

Women come up to me on the platform and say, "I want you to pray for my husband. He's sitting over there. He didn't want to come up, and he's having trouble."

I want to say, "Yes, he has a big problem standing in front of me right now."

When people rally support against someone by gossiping about him, that person has to believe God ten times harder because his friends and relatives are "cursing" him by what they say.

People even curse themselves! "Ever since I received Jesus, the devil won't leave me alone," someone will complain. It's a curse!

How To Hedge Your Life

Unless we decide to embrace God's perfect will, we're only going to get partial ministry or partial deliverance, always picking up our old "baggage" of unbelief again.

However, if we put the Word of the Lord in our heart and our mouth, we'll have God's best operating on our behalf. Ecclesiastes 10:8 says, "He that diggest a pit shall fall into it; and whoso breaketh an hedge, a serpent shall bite him." You can "hedge" your life and garrison it around by cooperating with God's Word.

This should be your confession:

"I'm strong in the Lord and in the power of His might. I've got the armor of God on, and my angels work overtime. I'm a winner. God always leads me to victory. I stand on

God's Word. I am not moved by circumstances. I don't go by what I see.

"I believe the Word of God. I'm not going to charge Him foolishly; I'm going to put His Word in my mouth. I'm not going to forget His benefits. He forgives all my iniquities, heals all my diseases, and then He satisfies my mouth with good things so my youth is renewed like the eagles'."

How To Combat Premature Aging

People at 40 years of age are getting old. You've got no business getting old at 40.

A wrong confession is:

"I must be getting old, ha-ha. This body isn't what it used to be. My memory is slipping. I can't remember like I used to." This is a curse.

When Caleb was 85 he said, "As my strength was, so it is now." Why was this? Because Caleb didn't spend his time in the desert griping about how he had missed out on entering the land of promise. He spent his life in the desert saying, "When all of you doubters die, I'm going over Jordan, and I'm going to possess the land!" And he did just that!

Put God's blessings in your mouth, and they'll find a way to your heart.

Blessings and Cursings

Let's see what else James has to say on the power of the tongue:

Therewith bless we God, even the Father; and therewith curse we men, which are made after the similitude of God.

Out of the same mouth proceedeth blessing and cursing. My brethren, these things ought not so to be.

James 3:9,10

Why not? Because both blessing and cursing have power. We must understand that what we *say*, whether blessing or cursing, packs power. That's why all the patriarchs laid hands on their children and *blessed* them with corn, wine, sheep, cattle, and prophesied a destiny of blessings over their lives. *Words have power.*

This is what God *said* about the Church: "I will bless them that bless thee, and curse him that curseth thee..." (Genesis 12:3; Galatians 3:14).

People speak against the Church and Christians, saying we're not going to make it, we're a bunch of flakes, and so forth. When they do this, they're cursing themselves by what they speak, because God is going to fight for His people.

Bitter Water or Sweet?

Don't let your mouth become a fountain for "bitter water," as James describes it. Realize you've got power in you, and God put it there. This power will work by your simply agreeing with what God says with your words.

Doth a fountain send forth at the same place sweet water and bitter?

Can the fig tree, my brethren, bear olive berries? either a vine, figs? so can no fountain both yield salt water and fresh.

James 3:11,12

What is James saying? He's saying, "If you are a righteous man or woman, choose to relay your identity by a good message. Let your words speak loudly on God's behalf."

The day will come when ordinary, everyday, Spirit-filled, Bible-believing Christians will do greater miracles than Jesus did two thousand years ago. And you're probably one of those Christians!

"Well, I *am* one of them."

Then do what you're told.

With our words we bind the devil. With our words we release God's will. With our words we bind circumstances that God didn't send. With our words we're going to get souls saved. With our words we're going to get the sick healed. And with a shout, we're going to get the dead raised

— because God has invested His glory in the heart of His children!

The Key to Right Standing

This is the key to right standing with God, found in the Book of Titus.

Unto the pure all things are pure: but unto them that are defiled and unbelieving is nothing pure: but even their mind and conscience is defiled.

They profess that they know God; but in works they deny him, being abominable, and disobedient, and unto every good work reprobate.

Titus 1:15,16

Let's look at this passage more closely. "Unto the pure all things are pure." Who are the pure? The Bible says that we purify our souls by obeying the truth. The Bible says to cleanse your hands and purify your hearts.

Positionally, purity of heart is a free gift Jesus gave. We didn't have to do anything to earn it. When we received Jesus and believed in the blood, we were pure instantly.

Why, then, is God saying some are pure and some are defiled? Just because you are positionally pure does not mean you're *keeping* yourself pure by what you say. By your words you are condemned, and by your words you are justified, and the Bible says the tongue can defile the whole body.

What the Pure Say

"To the pure, all things are pure." That means the pure talk purity. The pure talk about how wonderful it is to be washed in the blood. The pure talk about how wonderful it is to be friends with God. The pure say, "God is my Helper. I will not fear." The pure brag on God.

The pure realize the gift they have, and they allow it to be in their heart and mouth. What is this gift? It is the word of faith which we preach. The pure allow the Word to captivate their mouth.

On the other hand, the defiled and the unbelieving have defiled their own life by what they put in their mouth. When people who are saved and washed by the blood speak words contrary to what God has to say, it can stain and affect the garments they're wearing, because they are yielding their conscience, mind, and tongue to the wrong inspiration, and the words they speak end up defiling them.

Do you think you can talk any way you like and stay free from being defiled? You can't. The only way to stay free is, "You shall know the truth, and the truth shall make you free." *Put the truth into your mouth!*

We just read in verse 15, "...but unto them that are defiled and unbelieving is nothing pure." Why are they defiled and unbelieving? Because they're talking unbelief all the time. If they would talk the Word, it would bring faith, because faith comes by hearing the Word.

Why You're Losing Your Strength

When you talk about what the devil is doing and how hard your life is, you will find your strength draining out of you. When you start examining secular news reports, you will find yourself losing strength. When you get around the wrong person and let him or her talk long enough, you will find yourself drained and losing strength.

There is nothing pure in the unbelieving and the defiled. Their mind and their conscience is defiled. Instead of yielding themselves to the Word of God and being transformed by the renewing of their mind, they're yielding themselves to the word of the devil and letting their mind be captivated by a spirit of doubt and unbelief.

Paul wrote to Timothy, "For God hath not given us a spirit of fear; but of power, and of love, and of a sound mind" (2 Timothy 1:7).

Jesus said, "Now ye are clean through the word which I have spoken unto you" (John 15:3). The Word can and will cleanse you, and God tells us to keep ourselves clean in this way.

The Word Remains

As you read this book, there is a spiritual force present with you that can transform you and remain with you every day of your life. That force is the Word of God. No one can steal the Word you have learned; it's there to stay in your life.

As an exercise in hiding God's Word in your heart, read Psalm 91 as follows, noting that personal pronouns were substituted throughout, to make the Psalm more personal to you.

He that dwelleth in the secret place of the most High shall abide under the shadow of the Almighty.

I will say of the Lord, He is my refuge and my fortress: my God; in him will I trust.

Surely he shall deliver me from the snare of the fowler, and from the noisome pestilence.

He shall cover me with his feathers, and under his wings shall I trust: his truth shall be my shield and buckler.

I shall not be afraid for the terror by night; nor for the arrow that flieth by day;

Nor for the pestilence that walketh in darkness; nor for the destruction that wasteth at noonday.

A thousand shall fall at my side, and ten thousand at my right hand; but it shall not come nigh me.

Only with my eyes shall I behold and see the reward of the wicked.

Because I have made the Lord, which is my refuge, even the most High, my habitation;

There shall no evil befall me, neither shall any plague come nigh my dwelling.

For he shall give his angels charge over me, to keep me in all my ways.

They shall bear me up in their hands, lest I dash my foot against a stone.

I shall tread upon the lion and adder: the young lion and the dragon shall I trample under feet.

Because I have set my love upon him, therefore will he deliver me: he will set me on high, because I have known his name.

I shall call upon him, and he will answer me; he will be with me in trouble; he will deliver me, and honour me.

With long life will he satisfy me, and shew me his salvation.

Psalm 91

A Word of Blessing

In the Name of Jesus Christ, the King of kings and the Lord of lords, I pronounce over your life a word of blessing.

I declare that you are blessed and not cursed. I declare that you are free and not bound.

I pronounce that you are healed and not sick, joyful and not afflicted, an overcomer and not defeated, strong and not weak.

I declare that your mind is not in confusion, but you have the mind of Christ.

I declare that your prayers have not been neglected, but God is at work to answer you.

I declare that the Lord is ever present, and He is a source of help in time of need.

I decree now, in Jesus' Name, that every deep-planted root that has been the result of a word curse, a negative declaration that men have spoken over you, doctrine, religion, or false interpretation of the Word, every word that you may have spoken over yourself, every idea that the devil may have put into your mind, is uprooted in the Name of Jesus.

I release the proper self-image into your mind, because our image is Jesus, who is the image of God. And the Word says that we can look unto Him with an open face, and we can be changed into the *same* image, from glory to glory!

53

In the Name of Jesus Christ, the Son of God, I release on your life the fullness of His visitation, a double portion of His anointing.

And in the Name of Jesus, I declare that your life will be changed from this moment on. You are a warrior. You are victorious. *You are more than a conqueror.*

In Jesus' Name, I break off you everything that has hindered and limited you, and I release you in the Name of the Lord, that your self-image will rise into the likeness of Jesus, and the Greater One will begin to manifest, for you are not going under in defeat, and you are not unwanted.

You have come to Him, and He will not cast you out. The Lord is going to hold your hands up in victory, strength is going to be appropriated into your life, you are going to delight in the Lord, and He is going to give you the desires of your heart!

Chapter 5
The Keys to the Kingdom

A man's belly shall be satisfied with the fruit of his mouth; and with the increase of his lips shall he be filled.

Death and life are in the power of the tongue: and they that love it shall eat the fruit thereof.

Proverbs 18:20,21

Notice, a man's belly is not only filled in the natural; it is also filled spiritually. What is being discussed here is not the food part of your belly — the part you feed with natural bread — but the part you feed by the Word of God.

The Bible tells us, "The spirit of man is the candle of the Lord, searching all the inward parts of the belly" (Proverbs 20:27). By "the spirit of man," God is referring to the hidden man of the heart.

What you say will either starve or feed your spirit man. When you run around saying, "I'm weak," your spirit man will respond. When you run around saying, "I'm a sinner," your spirit man will respond. When you run around saying, "I don't know what I'm going to do; I'm so confused," your spirit man will respond.

Satisfaction and Contentment Can Be Yours

On the other hand, our text says that your belly will be satisfied by the fruit of your lips. That means internal satisfaction and contentment is not only the by-product of your hearing the Word; it's the by-product of your putting the Word in your mouth.

The phrase "with the increase of his lips shall he be filled" means this: For you to overflow with God's blessing to the point where you've got joy, strength, steadfastness, and stability — where you are an overcomer, have authority, and the devil fears you and can't touch you — you've got to fill not only your heart with the Word of God, but your mouth as well. Then, as the Word overflows out of you, it will begin to affect your body.

Neurosurgeons have discovered that there is a portion of the brain that adheres to what you speak. Therefore, when you say, "I am weak," that part of your brain will hear the command given to it by your will, and through your authority; and that central part of your brain will, in turn, send a message to the rest of your body, telling it to respond to the confession you gave it with your own mouth.

Although neurosurgeons are discovering this today, God said it thousands of years ago: "Death and life are in the power of the tongue: and they that love it [speaking of life] shall eat the fruit thereof." As we stated earlier, some people's big problems are the by-product of their big mouths!

Line Up Your Words With the Word

God brings life into your heart; however, that life will never explode into the rest of your makeup — transforming your mind, strengthening your soul, healing your body, and directing the course of your life properly — unless you begin to line up what you're saying with the Word of God.

Now look at Proverbs 15:13: "A merry heart maketh a cheerful countenance; but by sorrow of the heart the spirit is broken." Notice what is being said here: "A merry heart maketh a cheerful countenance." What does that mean?

It means if your heart is right with God, your face will show it. It means you can't help but be affected externally by how God affected you internally. You can't help it, because when your heart is happy, your countenance will be joyous.

How To Make Your Heart Happy

Do you know how to make your heart happy? The Bible says, "Trust in the Lord with all your heart." Your heart will never be at peace, be strong, or be without trouble unless you have made the decision to trust in the Lord. And your heart will never trust in the Lord unless you've made the decision to act on the Word of God.

Yes, you can hear the Word, but if you haven't made the decision to *act* on it, your heart will still be troubled. Jesus said, "Let not your heart be troubled...." That means, the moment I hear the Word and say, "Yes, I'm a doer of the Word — I'm going to do it, I'm going to act on it, I'm going to trust in it, God is my source" — I've trusted Him with all my heart. And when I do, my heart is happy. Why? Because it's heard good news.

Do you know the Bible is good news? The Bible *is* good news, so when I open it and read it, it tells me good things. Good things, in turn, reflect light on my spirit man, my heart, and my heart responds with joy to good news. And when my heart responds with joy to good news, my faith gets affected.

So it is true: "A merry heart maketh a cheerful countenance; but by sorrow of the heart the spirit is broken."

People Who Won't Hope

Have you ever met people who won't even hope? Have you ever met people who say, "Well, I just don't want to be disappointed again"? What happened to them? Their spirit was broken.

But don't blame it on God, and don't even blame it on the devil. Why do people lose their confidence, their faith, their commitment, and their spiritual "punch" in God? It's as Proverbs 15:13 says, "by sorrow of the heart the spirit is broken."

When a person chooses to hear a pessimistic report rather than God's optimistic report, that person will consequently end up with a broken spirit. Because his spirit will sorrow, his heart will sorrow. And not only will his faith lose its shine and its joy; his spirit will eventually be broken.

The result is a person walking around like a zombie. You can't get him to act on any of the Word of God.

The Liberating Knowledge of the Truth

The Bible says there is a group of people who will be ever learning, but will never be able to come to the knowledge of the truth. What is "the knowledge of the truth"?

The knowledge of the truth is simply that you don't have to wait another day to get the victory into your life. The knowledge of the truth is simple: If you hear it *and believe it*, that settles it. What you hear will give you the power to perform.

Now look at Proverbs 15:15: "All the days of the afflicted are evil; but he that is of a merry heart hath a continual feast." This is awesome! What does the afflicted *say*? The afflicted says, "Well, if my days weren't evil, I wouldn't be afflicted."

The Problem With Affliction

The Bible says, "The reason his days are evil is because he's afflicted." Why are his days evil? Because he's running around talking "Affliction, affliction, affliction, affliction." That's why he keeps running into evil days. And he says, "Well, if God would just take away the evil days, I wouldn't be afflicted." But God says, "If you'd stop being afflicted, you'd overcome the evil days."

Yes, the Bible does say, "Many are the afflictions of the righteous..." (Psalm 34:19), but it never says, "Let the righteous be afflicted," "Let the righteous talk affliction," or "Let the righteous put affliction on their lips."

Instead, it says, "but the Lord delivereth him out of them all." So the righteous will go through affliction, but God is not saying, "Affliction, affliction, affliction"; He's saying, "Deliverance, deliverance, deliverance! Victory, victory, victory!"

Because God says that, the righteous passes through an evil day only to end up in a brighter day. "But the path of the just is as the shining light, that shineth more and more unto the perfect day" (Proverbs 4:18).

So I'm not stating you won't run into trouble, but that trouble will be a stepping stone to breakthroughs. I'm not stating you won't run into obstacles, but those obstacles will be a stepping stone to breakthroughs.

What a Pessimist Says

The Lord says, "Don't put affliction in your mouth." Why? The afflicted will live all his days in evil *because he's talking evil.* He's giving the evil one power and dominion over his life to keep afflicting him by what he's putting in his mouth.

He's a pessimist. He's the one who says, "If anything can go wrong, it will!" He's the one who says, "My God, what's going to go wrong *next?*" He's the one who says, "God never answers my prayer." He's the one who says, "I can't wait to go to heaven, because it's sure been hell down here!" He's that guy. Avoid him. His days are evil because he's afflicted.

But look again at the man described in Proverbs 15:15: "...he that is of a merry heart hath a continual feast." He does, doesn't he? In the natural, people will say, "Of course he's happy, because he's having a feast all the time."

A Happy Feast

No! He's happy all the time *because he's choosing to feast on the Word of God.* That's what the Bible says. We just read it in our text, that a man's belly shall be satisfied with the fruit of his mouth.

Why is he having a feast? Because he's feeding on the Word of God. What is in his mouth is a good report. He's saying, "Hallelujah," and his heart is rejoicing.

The Word of God — which is spirit and life — is going into his spirit man and freeing him when affliction comes and he feels like he wants to speak the circumstances. Instead, he says no to the circumstances and speaks the Word of God. It shoots out of his mouth like a weapon of war, bursting every yoke, because the anointing destroys the yoke.

People say, "I'm going to get excited when I get a break-through," but God says, "When you get excited about my Word, a breakthrough is inevitable."

Some say, "Well, I'm going to serve God when I have more time," but God says, "Serve Me now, with the time you have, and I'll give you more time to serve Me later." Reverse the order.

"Well, if things would start going right, I'd get happy."

But God says, "If you'd get happy about the Word of God rather than things, things will line up with the Word of God." In other words, as Jesus said, "Seek ye first the kingdom of God, and his righteousness; and all these things shall be added unto you" (Matthew 6:33).

A Healthy Tongue

The Bible says, "A merry heart doeth good like a *medicine*" (Proverbs 17:22). Why? Because "the tongue of the wise is *health*" (Proverbs 12:18), and because God "sent His Word and *healed* them" (Psalm 107:20).

Therefore, when a person meditates on what God says, his heart will get happy about the Word of God, and he will put the Word in his mouth and speak it. And when he does, it will be health to all his being.

There are people who are sick because of what they *say*. They have ulcers because of how they talk. There are people whose serious diseases came upon them because they violated such simple principles in God's Word as, "Let not your heart be troubled..." (John 14:1).

They would not lean on God with all their heart. They allowed their heart to be tormented, and they stayed up nights, worrying and meditating about their "mountain" rather than looking to the God who moves mountains.

They *said*, "Look how big the mountain is!" and the more they talked abut it, the sicker their inner man got. And the sicker their inner man got, the more afflicted their body got.

Before they knew it, they were tormented by a disease they brought on themselves through the words they spoke. That's why the Bible says, "A merry (or happy) heart doeth good like a medicine."

Your Right To Be Sick and Miserable

Some will say, "Oh, leave me alone. I have every right to be mad!"

Then you also have every right to be *sick*, every right to be *afflicted*, every right to be *tormented*, every right to be *defeated*, every right to *go broke*, and every right to *fall* by the wayside — because you can't violate what God said and end up victorious.

Nothing happens by chance. That's why Jesus did not say, "You're lucky." He said, "You're *blessed.*" That means "fortunate and to be envied."

Some people around me get envious of the things God does for me, but what He does for me is biblical. When you begin to invest in what God said and to build on the rock, things line up and work out for you.

Because your friends haven't made the same sacrifice and decision to go God's way, they yield through their weakness to the spirit that influences envy.

Guard yourself by what you say, because your words are filled with the power of Almighty God!

God's Winning Principle

First Peter 3:10 is very significant:

For he that will love life, and see good days, let him refrain his tongue from evil, and his lips that they speak no guile.

At first glance, this verse may seem superficial. But if you look at it again, you will find the principle that God wove throughout the Old and New Covenants.

This is what He is literally saying in verse 10: "If you love life and you want to see good days [both are *future* conditions], you ought to refrain your tongue *now* from evil and your lips *now* that they speak no guile."

The primary causes of deaths among our teenaged population are drug- and alcohol-related accidents. Why? Teenagers don't love life. Why not? Because the modern world has conditioned them to believe that life is not worthy to be loved.

The lyrics of rock music have taught them that death is better than life. This message has been repeated in the evil reports they have heard, in the loose and rebellious lifestyles their parents lived in the '60s, and in their peers' insistence that drugs and alcohol are the best ways to escape reality and the seemingly insurmountble problems in their young lives.

Yes, reality can stress you if you let it. Reality can weigh you down and break you down if you let it. If you don't walk by the authority of Jesus Christ, there is no victory in the world. That's why Jesus said to His disciples, "...be of good cheer; *I have overcome the world*" (John 16:33).

When Jesus said those words, He had not yet overcome the world — but notice He used the past tense: "I *have overcome* the world."

He had not yet gone to the cross. Did you know He went to the cross by faith? He said, "I could ask my Father right now for twelve legions of angels, and they would deliver me" (Matthew 26:53).

He had not yet gone to the grave — and until that time, no one had been resurrected from the grave in a glorified body. He was doing it all by faith.

The Bible says that Jesus was "the author and finisher of our faith; who for the joy that was set before him endured the cross..." (Hebrews 12:2). So Jesus had to fight the good fight of faith the way we fight it!

The Power of Words

Why, then, would He say, "be of good cheer; I have overcome the world"? Because Jesus was well aware of the power of words, and He was continually setting His life in motion in accordance with what God said.

Jesus didn't even fight the devil without the Word of God. Instead, He told him repeatedly, "It is written...it is written...it is written." He didn't say, "I think I heard it somewhere"; He said, "It is written!" That means He read the Book. He knew what it said.

The second major cause of teenaged deaths is suicide. Why? They don't love life. You can't love life and kill yourself. If you live by the Word of God, you're having too much fun to die!

It's fun to beat the devil up. It's fun to walk in divine health. It's fun to be happy. It's fun to be a Christian. It's fun to be Spirit filled. It's fun to be a winner. It's fun to serve Jesus. It's fun to be the head and not the tail. It's fun to be the repairer of the breach. You're having too much fun to die!

The Devil's Ancient Weapon

Why are teenagers killing themselves? As we noted earlier, the lyrics of rock music are seducing some of them to commit suicide. *There is power in words* — something the devil has known and capitalized on since the Garden of Eden.

As a matter of fact, he capitalized on the power of words even before the garden, because the Bible says his tail drew a third of the angels of heaven into rebellion against God (Revelation 12:4). He must have preached a sermon to them, saying, "I will be like the Most High. Follow me!"

Words have been in existence from the creation and even before, and the forces of both light and darkness have both used them.

In the Garden of Eden, Satan taunted Adam and Eve with his *words:* "Hath God said?" and those words caused man to fall. Every human being on earth today is experiencing the fall that those few words in the garden produced. *Words!*

Look again at First Peter 3:10:

For he that will love life [in the future], **and see good days** [that he hasn't seen yet], **let him refrain his tongue** [now] **from evil, and his lips** [now] **that they speak no guile."**

Creating Your World Through Words

No one commits to divorce just like that. No one becomes an alcoholic just like that. No one kills someone just like that. No one commits suicide just like that. They've been set up throughout the course of their life to act in error by *what they said.*

They started early on by saying, "Boy, life is the pits. This is hell. I guess that's my cross to bear." Some people talk about the cross more than the resurrection. "Well, you know, I'm carrying big burdens," they sigh.

If you keep talking about your burdens, this attitude will grow and fester in you. Before you know it, you won't like life.

You'll wake up one morning and think that the world is getting grayer every day. All the color seems to have gone out of the world, and it doesn't look the same to you anymore.

Life used to be a playground to you; now it's a battlefield — *created by your own words.*

"Well, the fight is hard, brother. Pray for me so I can hold on." If you keep talking like that, my prayers won't do you any good. It's like saying, "Grease my grip."

Don't Rent Your Tongue to the Devil

However, if you want to love life, notice what Jesus said in John 10:10, "The thief cometh not, but for to steal, and to kill, and to destroy: I am come that they might have life, and that they might have it more abundantly."

The devil will try to steal God's Word by taking it out of your mouth and inserting another word there. He will try to take a good report out of your mouth and replace it with a wrong report.

Why? Because he knows he'll abort God's will in your life if he succeeds. Don't put your tongue up for rent! Just say, "No vacancies!"

Whether you end up loving or hating life, or seeing good or evil days in the future depends on whether you refrain your tongue now from evil and your lips now that they speak no guile.

What is evil? Anything that the Word doesn't say. The most subtle religious phrase could be a stench in the nostrils of God. It could look perfectly proper, yet it still could be a stench in the nostrils of God if it's not sanctioned by the living Word of God.

Camouflaged in Angels' Wings

Evil, you see, is not necessarily a hideous creature that we can all discern without hesitation. Evil can come camouflaged in angels' wings. The Bible warns us against:

...false apostles, deceitful workers, transforming themselves into the apostles of Christ.

And no marvel; for Satan himself is transformed into an angel of light.

2 Corinthians 11:13,14

Some will argue, "I believe God. I trust Him."

You've got to have wisdom, too, and learn to discern spiritual things.

If you love life and want to see good days, then, refrain your tongue from evil — and don't put guile in your mouth. Guile is anything that's not the truth.

Therefore, if you put the truth in your mouth, you shall know the truth, and the truth shall make you free. And you shall be free from every weapon the devil can use against you.

Be a Good Steward of Your Words

Remember, the Bible says that we shall all appear before the Judgment Seat of Christ. We are going to give an account of the things done in our body, according to Second Corinthians 5:10. And in Matthew 12:36, Jesus said that we are also going to give an account of every idle word that we speak!

Can you see the need for good stewardship over how we talk? It is important not only how our message reflects the Word of God, but also how it reflects the right spirit. What does that mean? Paul says, make sure you're speaking by the right spirit!

We having *the same spirit of faith,* according as it is written, I have believed, and therefore have I spoken; we also believe, and therefore speak.

2 Corinthians 4:13

When you are speaking by the same spirit of faith, you are going to speak words of faith in God. You are going to speak confidence in God.

You are not going to speak a hazy, uncertain message. You are not going to act as if you don't know where you are going. You are not going to believe in a mysterious God no one can second guess, or a God you can't count on to help you.

Speaking by the Spirit of Faith

When you speak by the same spirit of faith, you're speaking about a God who said out of His own mouth — which cannot lie — "I will never leave thee, nor forsake thee...lo, I am with you alway" (Hebrews 13:5; Matthew 28:20).

Jesus said, "Fear not." You can count on God. He will never disappoint you. And since He is with you all the time, you have nothing to fear.

Know what God's function is when He is with you. Suppose you had a friend who said, "I'm with you," but when you got in a fight, he just stood there and said, "Don't worry; I'm with you" — and he watched your opponent beat you up!

The next time you fought, you'd discourage your so-called friend's presence. You'd say to him, "Thanks very much, but I'd rather not have you here this time, so you won't have anything to talk about."

God isn't like your fickle friend. He's not with you just to stand by idly and watch you get beaten up by your problems; He's there to do something about them. He says, "Don't fear. Count on Me to do something about your circumstances every time you encounter difficulties. Count on Me!"

Beware of Hyperfaith?

Someone will argue, "I appreciate that — it's wonderful — but, of course, I don't want to get into hyperfaith. I love the faith message, but of course we've got to steer clear of that *hyperfaith* stuff."

I looked up "hyper" in the dictionary, and it defined it as "extreme, overabundant." You can't get hyper enough for God, hallelujah! You can't go too far for God! In fact, you can't go *far enough* for God!

That's like saying, "Don't trust in God too much. Don't get hyperfaith to where you have an overabundant, extreme trust in the Lord."

How many know some backslidden, lukewarm theologian came up with that statement? Never base your theology on mere circumstances.

You demand, "I've tried faith before, and it didn't work, so I left it alone. Why didn't it work?"

Go to the Word and find out. You can't build your life on an old cliche.

The Bible assures us that the Lord is "a friend that sticketh closer than a brother" (Proverbs 18:24). You may safely trust in the Lord with all of your heart!

God's Master Plan

People say, "Well, you never know what God is going to do."

I'll tell you what He's going to do: He's going to help His people, and He's going to build a Church that the gates of hell shall not, cannot, will not prevail against.

Jesus told His disciples in Matthew 16:18:

...I will build my church, and the gates of hell shall not prevail against it.

What is Jesus telling us here? He is saying, "If You will let Me build you, I'll make you so strong, you won't fear the gates of hell. You will be built by God. And when the enemy attacks you, hell can't overcome you, because when I build something, I build it right!"

Then, in Matthew 16:19, Jesus said:

And I will give unto thee the keys of the kingdom of heaven: **and whatsoever thou shalt bind** [or disallow] **on earth shall be bound** [or disallowed] **in heaven: and whatsoever thou shalt loose** [or allow] **on earth, shall be loosed** [or allowed] **in heaven.**

Using Words To Bind and Loose

Do you know how to bind? Do you know you use your lips, your words, to bind?

Jesus said, "I'm giving you the keys that release the kingdom of God and its invading force in the earth — and *those keys I'm putting in your mouth.* You bind and say no, and it's so. You loose it and say yes, and it's so."

You can find all the laws for binding and loosing in the Word of God, and you can also find the faith needed to do it correctly by *hearing* the Word of God.

If someone hears an unbelieving minister say from the pulpit, "Some of you are going to have a heart attack, because sometimes it's God will that you be sick," that person is not going to have the right kind of faith to stand against such a lie from the devil.

But not everyone falls for such words of unbelief, and these are the winners who are coming on the scene!

Chapter 6

Words at Work

And as Jesus passed by, he saw a man which was blind
from his birth.

And his disciples asked him, saying, Master, who did sin,
this man, or his parents, that he was born blind?

Jesus answered, Neither hath this man sinned, nor his
parents: but that the works of God should be made manifest in him.

I must work the works of him that sent me, while it is
day: the night cometh, when no man can work.

As long as I am in the world, I am the light of the world.

John 9:1-5

Let's set the scene here: As the disciples were out walking with the Lord one day, they passed a man who had been
blind from birth.

There are certain conditions, such as blindness, that have
been around for a long time, and if they continue to go
unchecked and unchallenged, they will continue to be a
stronghold; they will never change.

As they walked past the blind man, the disciples turned
and asked Jesus, "Who sinned — *this* man or his parents —
that he was born blind?" They didn't say "that" man, so they
must have been right next to the man when they asked the
question.

He was born blind, but he wasn't born deaf, so he could
hear what the disciples were saying. What does that have to
do with anything? Don't forget, words are very important.

Jesus said, "Be careful what you hear. Don't give everything a hearing ear." Sometimes you can't keep from hearing certain things, but that doesn't mean you have to give them "a hearing ear." This means, don't get too impressed when the devil is talking pessimism, skepticism, and all those other things he likes to peddle. Don't say politely, "Oh, is that so?"

Who Sinned?

The disciples asked a common question: "Did this man sin, or did his parents sin, that he was born blind?"

But how could you sin *before* you were born and consequently be struck blind?

There was a prominent theology in those days that not only taught correctly that the sins of the father are transferred to the son, but also taught incorrectly that a person could sin while in his mother's womb.

If you come from an ungodly family background, the devil will try to attach onto you the habits, diseases, sicknesses, poverty spirits, and anything else he can from your evil forbears.

"What should I do about it?"

Just say, "Devil, I'm a brand-new creature. I'm part of a new family now. Cancer doesn't run in this family. High blood pressure doesn't run in this family. Poverty doesn't run in this family. Insanity doesn't run in this family." By saying this, you terminate that family weakness.

It's Time To Throw Away Your "Religion"

I want you to get the picture: This blind man was around crowds all his life, and ever since he was an infant he heard people whispering, "I wonder who sinned, this blind boy or his parents? God is trying to teach them something. I wonder why he's in that predicament? Oh, well, God moves in mysterious ways..."

That erroneous theology was the stronghold of the devil in the blind man's life. There are theological strongholds in many Christians' lives today, too. Some Christians need to throw away their "religion"! They would get happy if they did.

"Who did sin, this man or his parents?"

In the original Greek, there is no division of verses; you don't stop at verse 3 and then start verse 4. You read the passage this way: "Jesus answered, Neither hath this man sinned, nor his parents: but that the works of God should be made manifest in him. I must work the works of him that sent me...."

Later translators were the ones who chose to divide this passage into separate verses, changing its meaning.

Then some theologians decided, "See, Jesus said, 'Neither has this man sinned, nor his parents: but that the works of God should be made manifest in him.'" They added, "Sometimes the work of God is to be born blind."

Do you know what that tells me? The blind are leading the blind, because that's *not* what Jesus said! He said, "No, this man did not sin, and neither did his parents sin; *but so that the works of God would be made manifest in him, I must do the works of him that sent me.*"

What was Jesus talking about? The opening of blinded eyes was the work of God! The working of miracles was the work of God!

God's Words Bring Faith

The blind man, for the first time in his life, *heard words that were sent by God.* He was sitting by the roadside, and he couldn't see, but he could hear. He heard some men ask a rabbi, "Did this blind man sin, or did his parents sin? Why is he blind?" And then he heard the rabbi reply, "No, this man did not sin; neither did his parents." *Hope sprang up in his heart.*

He thought, "What! Do you mean to tell me I'm not blind because God is trying to teach me something? Do you mean I'm not struggling to make ends meet because God wants to keep me humble? Do you mean the circumstances I'm in right now are not sanctioned, ordained, and appointed by God?"

The moment you get a grip on reality, hope will spring up in you! Your hands will no longer be tied.

You may be in an evil day, but you don't have to live there for the rest of your life.

You may be in a time of need, but it's not going to continue like that for the rest of your life.

You may be encountering affliction or resistance, but the Lord will deliver you out of all of those situations.

Set Free by the Truth

The first step in the blind man's healing was that he heard the truth. What was the truth? It came to him *in the form of words*. Jesus *said*, "No, he did not sin; neither did his parents sin." The man's faith sprang up. He felt better about himself. Ever since he could remember, he felt like something was wrong with him. He felt like God held something against him. He felt like the Lord chose to make him a blind beggar because He was displeased with him.

But now, for the first time in his life, he was excited. He hadn't even heard about miracles. He hadn't even heard about what Jesus wanted to do for him. But the moment he heard that neither he nor his parents had sinned, he felt better about himself.

That tells me it's important to hear the truth about yourself. However, that doesn't mean you should pray like this: "Well, God, You know I'm a nobody, and in all the humility I can muster, I just want You to know that I understand that You don't have to answer my prayer. But if You see fit, in your divine sovereignty to intervene, here am I."

God says, "I'm not even listening, if you're taking that attitude."

The truth is, you *are* a somebody. Jesus redeemed you! He bought all of us nobodies back and began to work on us to transform us into His image.

So it's not up to God to decide whether or not He wants to answer you; it's up to you, in the way you approach Him. If you don't believe in Him, He can't answer you. If you don't believe He will, He can't.

Yes, sometimes He'll violate the normal order and intervene — sometimes you'll see the sovereignty of God — but you won't see it every day, and you can't be sure that God will exercise His sovereignty in every situation. After all, the Bible says, "The just shall live by *faith*."

When you approach God, bear in mind that He gives freely and generously to all. He is not a respecter of persons. He will give to everyone who approaches Him in faith. When you know that, and when you know the kind of nature God has, you will know the kinds of things God does.

The Light of the World

Jesus said, "But that the works of God should be made manifest in him [the blind man], I must work the works of him that sent me while it is day; the night cometh when no man can work. As long as I am in the world, I am the light of the world."

Later, Jesus said that *you* are the light of the world. Why? Because He is no longer in the world bodily; He is in the world through the Body of Christ. This means He is now in the world through us, so we have become the light of the world.

The Bible says, "Let your light so shine before men, that they may see your works, and glorify your Father which is in heaven" (Matthew 5:16).

What is the light? The light is the Word of God, because "The entrance of thy words giveth light" (Psalm 119:130).

What is the result of light? The works of God. When you hear and believe the Word, you'll do the works. When you hear the Word, it brings the light. When the light comes, it brings the strength. And when the strength comes, you do the work.

Someone Sent the Rabbi

Now, the blind man was sitting there listening to what was going on around him. The first thing he heard was that neither he nor his parents had sinned. The second thing he heard from Jesus was, "As long as I am in the world, I am the light of the world. I must work the works of him that sent me, while it is day."

Another thing this blind man heard for the first time was that someone sent this rabbi to do something about his condition. I ask people, "Do you believe God sent me here to heal you?"

Some say, "Yes." Some say, "I hope so." And some say, "I pray to God He did." That really doesn't make any sense. It doesn't matter how long you pray to God about it, because if He didn't send me, He didn't; and if He did, He did.

Receive the Prophet Correctly

I ask people this question because it's very important what people believe about the ministry gift. For example, if you don't receive a prophet in the way he should be received, he will just kick the dust off his feet and walk off. Where is he going? Someplace where they will receive him correctly!

The value and trust we put in what God said and the person He has anointed may determine whether or not He will visit us.

Remember, Jesus pointed out that there were many widows in Israel in the days of the prophet Elijah, but God sent him to someone who wasn't even a Jew. Then He reminded the people that there were many lepers in the days of the prophet Elisha, but God only sent Naaman the Syrian to him for healing (Luke 4:25-27).

When the blind man heard a sermon for the first time in his life, he heard the words, "Feel better about yourself. The One who sent Me, sent Me to do His works." And he knew one thing: He wasn't blind because God did it to him; his blindness was not the work of God.

He also knew that there was someone in the world who was the light of the world, and he was sent by someone else to do the works of that someone.

Therefore, the blind man concluded, if blindness was not the work of God, and he was not in sin, this rabbi must be getting ready to do something about his blindness!

Do you see how faith sprang up in the man's heart? And he got it *through words.* He got it because he *heard.* (Some people "hear" but never *hear.)*

Now look at what Jesus did next in John 9:

When he had thus spoken, he spat on the ground, and made clay of the spittle, and he anointed the eyes of the blind man with the clay,

And said unto him, Go, wash in the pool of Siloam, (which is by interpretation, Sent)....

John 9:6,7

Let's stop here and remember what He had said earlier: "I must work the works of him that sent me while it is day...As long as I am in the world, I am the light of the world."

What was that spitting sound? The blind man was sitting there thinking, "I didn't sin. My parents didn't sin. My blindness is not the work of God. This man was sent by someone to do his works. He's the light of the world — but now I hear spitting."

No Guarantee of Healing

Faith was springing up in the blind man. This rabbi was getting ready to do something. He put mud on the blind man's eyes and said, "Go, wash in the pool of Siloam" (the pool called "Sent").

Why didn't Jesus tell him, "You're going to come back seeing"? Because there was no guarantee he was going to come back seeing! *It all depended on how the blind man received the prophet.*

Remember the cleansing of the ten lepers? Why did only one come back to Jesus to give thanks? Why did Jesus continually tell people, "Your faith has made you whole; go and be healed of your plague."

Just because you got healed does not mean you are going to keep your healing. You must make a decision to lay hold on what God said and not let the devil or the circumstances of life steal it from you.

Jesus gave the blind man this message in a roundabout way. He told him, "I'm the light of the world. I'm here to do the works of him that sent me while it is day." And He spat on the ground and put it on his eyes. It doesn't take a genius to figure out that His whole sermon had to do with the man's blind eyes.

Stepping Into a Different Realm

This knowledge is reality, and it will make winners out of us. I don't know about you, but I'm going to step into a different realm in the spirit every day with Jesus. I'm going to open blinded eyes more than I ever have before. I'm going to open deaf ears more than I ever have before.

The blind man's healing all started with words. Jesus *said,* "As long as I'm here, I'm going to do something." He spat on the ground, and put mud on the man's eyes. The blind man was probably thinking, "Now where is the pool of Siloam?" I'm sure it was quite a distance from where they were.

Why didn't Jesus just say, "Open!" Because sometimes you need to be given adequate time to meditate on what you have *heard.*

Rehearsing Jesus' Words

As this blind man was going to the pool, what was thinking about? Every word that Jesus had spoken to him was being rehearsed in every part of his being, all the way to the pool.

"I didn't sin. My parents didn't sin. I'm not blind because it's the work of God. I heard someone who was sent by someone else to do the works of that someone. He put something on my eyes and told me to wash at the pool. Maybe this man was sent by God to open my eyes!"

Can you see the blind man's train of thought?

"Who sent you to the pool?"

"Someone who was sent by someone else."

"What did He tell you to do?"

"Go wash in the pool."

"What's the name of the pool?"

"Sent."

"Who sent you?"

"Someone who said I didn't sin."

"What else did He say?"

"My parents didn't sin."

"What else did He say?"

"My blindness is not the work of God."

"What else did He say?"

"He's going to do the work of God."

"Then what did He do?"

"Put mud on my eyes."

"What did He tell you to do?"

"He sent me."

"Where?"

"To the pool called 'Sent.'"

Words Bring Faith

What inspired that message of faith in him? *Words. Words. Words.* As he thought on the words of Jesus all the way to the pool, power, hope, and faith rose up on the inside of him.

I believe that before he even got to the pool, he thought, "Wait a minute! Wait a minute! I didn't sin...and my parents didn't sin...so I didn't deserve to be born blind. This is not the work of God...I've been hearing lies all along. Someone told me he came to do the works of him that sent him...then he sent me to the pool called 'Sent.' *My eyes are going to be opened, because He's the light of the world! I don't have to be blind!*"

And when he got to the pool, his faith was so high, the moment he put water on his eyes, he was ready to see. Why? Because *he had heard words that were power packed and charged.*

But the prophet of God had never said to him, "Go wash, and you are going to come back seeing." Jesus never said that to him!

Choosing To Believe

Skepticism has been around for thousands of years. The skeptics are still saying, "Well, the preacher told me to do such-and-such — *but it didn't happen!*"

The Word is alive. If that blind man had chosen to believe a lie, he would have ruined Jesus' reputation. He could have gone to that pool, washed, and returned blind — unchanged — saying, "I didn't believe You in the first place!"

The story would have spread far and wide. Who gets the blame for failure in the lives of people who hear the Word of God? The preacher!

People never admit, "I didn't believe the Word." Instead, they point to the preacher and say, "You said if I gave, it would be given to me, and it didn't happen. You said if I believed God, I would be healed, but I'm still sick. You said...you said...you said!"

Jesus is wise. He knew that the sower sows the seed, which is the Word, but He also knew that only 25 percent of what was sown would fall on good soil and grow. In His parable on the subject, He taught that some of the seed would fall on hard ground, some would be burned up, and some would be choked by weeds, or stolen.

So He said, "He that hath an ear to hear, let him hear." What was He talking about? He knew there were some who would not hear with a readiness to perceive and act on what they had heard. What did He recommend we do with such fallow ground? He said, "Break up your fallow ground."

We can't say our heart is hard because God made us that way. We must prepare our heart for a visitation of God. Then we can all be good ground.

Demanding Corresponding Action

When Jesus told the blind man, "Go wash," He did not say, "Go and you'll come back seeing" — *because it was up to the condition of the man's heart, readiness, and willingness to act on the Word to provide him with the miracle.*

Why send a blind man on a walk? Why demand of him corresponding action?

Sometimes I stand in the pulpit and tell sick people, "Shout 'glory'!" They won't do it, because Christians want miracles served to them on a silver platter.

They want to come to God's restaurant, but they don't want Him to spread a table before them. They expect Him to tie the napkin around their neck, cut their food for them, place it in their mouth, move their jaw up and down so they can chew it, and then force them to swallow! It's the truth.

What happens is, the Lord begins to demand of us a cor-responding action. Why? He's trying to get us to be blessed. *A corresponding action will always put us in a place where we're candidates to be blessed.*

We say, "Give God praise," but people won't do it. What they're saying, without really saying it, is, "My heart is

not in a place where I'm going to respond to what I'm hearing. I'm just here doing the 'religious' thing. I'm supposed
to come to church, so I've come."

Feeding the Word

The Lord asked Peter, "Do you love Me?"

"Yes."

"Then feed my sheep."

What was Peter supposed to feed us? *The Word.* That
meant he was to do the speaking, and the words which are lit-
eral spirit food, would go out to feed the lambs of God.

The Word of God would produce the strength and the
power of God in us, because God's power is in His Word. It
would produce God's authority through us *by what we said.*

However, we can short-circuit it just like that. We can
block God's power out of our life by yielding our tongue to
the wrong source.

If you believe that the Word of God is alive, if you love
life, and if you want to see good days, you must begin to
speak the right thing now.

Then you will begin to believe in a brighter day. You
will begin to believe in a victorious destiny. You will believe,
meditate, and think on God's goodness and provision. The
Bible calls it not only provision, but benefit: "Bless the Lord,
O my soul, and forget not all his benefits" (Psalm 103:2).

How God Inhabits Our Praises

The Bible also says that God inhabits the praises of His
people (Psalm 22:3). We always interpreted this as meaning
congregational praise. We lift up our hands in church and
begin to praise the Lord, and we say, "God inhabits (or lives
and dwells with and is enthroned upon) the praises of His
people."

But do you know what praise is? It's literally "to brag
on someone." That's what praise is! If I were to praise you,

I would tell you you're wonderful and you're the greatest. That's praise.

Remember, the Bible says there are some people who love the praise of men more than the praise of God. What is the praise? The uplifting. Praise doesn't happen only in church.

Let me show you where praise can be found. Suppose I run into a wall, and the devil says, "Look how *big* this wall is!"

I tell him, "My God is bigger than this wall. Greater is He that is in me that he that is in this wall. This wall is not even worthy of worrying about. This wall is getting ready to be blasted out of the way, because I'm a winner, not a loser. My God is with me always, and He's leading me through!"

Releasing God's Power

That's praise. God inhabits that praise! These words of praise release God's power out of the inside of me. And the more I'm convinced of my words, the quicker that wall shrinks, falls, splits, crumbles, and disappears!

Suppose I am walking through a desert, and someone says to me, "We all go through desert experiences. I'm in a desert experience in my own life."

But I begin to say, "My God makes a garden out of the desert, and when I pass through the valley of the shadow of death, I will fear no evil. When I pass through the valley of Baca, I'm going to make it a well (Psalm 84:6). I'm a voice crying in the wilderness, and He makes the desert to bloom."

When Praise Is Warfare

What am I doing? Praising God. Praise is easy when everything is going good, but *praise is warfare when everything is going wrong.*

This is what happens: As you begin to talk (praise), God inhabits your praises, and He begins to pour out of you. *The flood that's in your belly begins to flood the desert.* Before you know it, the desert changes. It begins to bloom, hallelujah!

So you praise God by what you say about Him, and you release His power through you by your confidence in Him. "Cast not away therefore your confidence, which hath great recompence of reward," Hebrews 10:35 says. Then the Bible teaches us in Galatians 6:9, "...in due season we shall reap, if we faint not." The Bible says that Jesus endured the cross for the joy that was set before Him:

Looking unto Jesus, the author and finisher of our faith; who for the joy that was set before him endured the cross, despising the shame, and is set down at the right hand of the throne of God.

Hebrews 12:2

The Bible teaches us to "lay aside every weight, and the sin which doth so easily beset us, and let us run with patience the race that is set before us" (Hebrews 12:1). We are to "consider him that endured such contradiction of sinners against himself, lest ye be wearied and faint in your minds" (Hebrews 12:3).

Don't Faint in Your Mouth!

The moment you faint in your mind, you will faint *in your mouth!* And the moment you faint in your mouth, you will release death and cursing rather than life and blessing.

The problem will come through what you consider. If you consider the problem, you will faint in your mind, and you will *talk the problem.*

On the other hand, if you consider God, you will be strengthened in your mind, and you will *talk the answer.*

You won't consider the lack; you will consider the Provider. You won't consider the circumstance; you will consider the God of the circumstance. You won't consider the hardship; you will consider the winner and the overcomer. It's all in what you consider.

If you keep meditating on the Word of God and believing and trusting in the Word of God, you will have strength in your mind, and life will come forth out of your mouth. The Bible says that you will learn to love life, and you will see good days.

Other books by Dr. Christian Harfouche

Authority Over the Powers of Darkness
Doing the Impossible
How To Receive Your Miracle
Living On The Cutting Edge
The Miracle Ministry of the Prophet
The Silver, The Gold, and The Glory
The Spirit Guide